An 'Ageing Well in your Community' conversation series was one prototype that emerged from a five-year qualitative research project called Innovative Age, conducted by The Australian Centre for Social Innovation (TACSI). Commissioned by the South Australian Office for Ageing Well, the project's intent was to deepen understanding of how we live as we age. I partnered with TACSI to co-design and test the conversation program structure with participants in Mount Barker, South Australia in 2018–2019. Over the last couple of years this conversation series has also been presented in other communities with long term positive impacts for participants and community.

At the start of the Covid pandemic, when the in-person conversations were not possible, I used the time to write this book: *Getting older—let's talk about it: a conversation guide to ageing well.* Each chapter in this book is a conversation topic I explore in the face-to-face program.

This book is designed specifically for Australians to prepare for their ageing futures or to support a family member or friend to age well in their community. It is practical, inclusive and affirming of the positives of the ageing process.

Lia Parsons
September 2022

Lia Parsons is a social activist in her mid-sixties, dedicated to tackling ageism and working collaboratively with older people to promote positive ageing. As an author, with a background in nursing and occupational therapy, she has professional knowledge and expertise combined with lived experience. This, her first book, documents what she does, both personally and professionally. She is passionately drawn to inform, support and encourage people to age well at home in their own communities. Her focus is on 'engaging with' instead of 'doing for' people. Her intention is to encourage and motivate each reader to take responsibility for their own future ageing years, their own living and dying, as she believes everyone intrinsically knows their own needs and understands their own wishes.

Getting Older

Let's talk about it!

A conversation guide to
ageing well in *your* community

LIA PARSONS

Published by Zest Creative – Living Life

Copyright © 2023. All rights reserved. No portion of this publication may be used, reproduced or transmitted by any means, digital, electronic, mechanical, photocopy or recording without written permission of the publisher, except in the case of brief quotations within critical articles or reviews.

The publisher has no responsibility for the persistence or accuracy of URLs for any external or third-party internet websites that are referred to in this publication, and does not guarantee that any content on such websites is or will remain accurate or appropriate.

ISBN: 978-0-6456940-0-0 (paperback)
ISBN: 978-0-6456940-1-7 (e-book)

First edition, 2023

Cover illustration by Sanne Kerssens

For book orders and enquiries, contact:
www.zestcreativeaustralia.com.au

A catalogue record for this work is available from the National Library of Australia

Dedication

To all who I met along my journey,
you who shaped my life and who taught me how to live it.
The conversations we have had, the learning I have done
and the changes I have made.
Thank you!

Contents

DEDICATION v
CONTENTS vii
PREFACE xi
INTRODUCTION xvii
    Ageing is not a problem or a disease—Ageing is living! xvii
    Topics of conversation xxii
CHAPTER 1. HOME, BELONGING AND COMMUNITY 1
    Home is where the heart is 10
        Artistic Activity 11
CHAPTER 2. THE REALITIES OF AGEING 13
        Scenario 1. 18
        Scenario 2. 18
        Scenario 3. 18
        Scenario 4. 19
CHAPTER 3. AGEISM 24
CHAPTER 4. MONEY MATTERS 35
        Activity 46
CHAPTER 5. CARE AND CARE SUPPORT 49
    Our current aged care model 63

CHAPTER 6. THE IMPORTANCE OF SOCIAL CONNECTIONS.................... 69
   Activity: Your social connections 73
  Social connections and the coronavirus pandemic 75
   Activity 80
   'Three good things' exercise 80
   'Flourishing or ageing well' exercise 81
  Looking at the bigger picture.. 81

CHAPTER 7. EMERGING AND ESTABLISHED HOUSING MODELS... 84
  What housing options do we currently have available? 92
   Retirement and lifestyle villages................................92
   Residential aged care 94
  Emerging alternative housing models 95
   Shared housing...98
   Homeshare...99
   The Henry Project..99
   Co-housing 100
   Senior co-housing specifically for people 60+ 101
   Activity 106
  Resources 107

CHAPTER 8. LIVING LIFE WITH MEANING AND PURPOSE......................... 109
   Tree of life 115
  Spirituality 120
   Activity: purposeful living 122
   Activity: Write a letter to your future self.................123

CHAPTER 9. PLANNING FOR END OF LIFE........................ 125
  Advance care plan and advance care directive....................... 128
  Power of attorney (POA) 131

Making a will 132
Organ or tissue donation.. 132
Organise and dispose of your 'stuff' 133
An emotional will.. 134
Place of death.. 135
    Dying in a hospital..135
    Dying in a hospice 136
    Dying in residential aged care/nursing home 137
    Dying at home 137
Palliative care 138
Death or end of life doulas 139
Euthanasia: voluntary assisted dying.............................. 139
Where to from here? 141
    Activity 141
    Artistic activity: fears and challenges,
    opportunities and courage 142
Resources 143
    Websites...143
    Recommended reading...144

CHAPTER 10. PLANNING FOR YOUR FUNERAL 145
What to consider when planning for your funeral 148
Who to notify when death occurs.................................. 148
Organ donation... 149
Choosing to go to a funeral home or to stay at home.... 150
Funeral arrangements 151
    Coffin or casket..153
    Green burials...153
    A shroud 154
    Notification...155
    Visiting and viewing...155

  Transporting the body..156
  The funeral service..156
  A wake 158
 Disposing of the body **158**
  Cemetery 158
  Cremation...159
  Aquamation 159
  Composting burial 160
 Final considerations... **160**
 Resources **163**
CHAPTER 11. COURAGE TO CHANGE:
   TO LIVE, AGE AND DIE WELL **165**
  Activity: Reflections...174
  Activity: thinking outside the box......................................175
CONCLUSION. ON YOUR WAY **176**
  Artistic activity 176
 Finally.. **177**
  Activity: planting the future 179
ACKNOWLEDGEMENTS... **181**
REFERENCES **183**
ENDNOTES **195**

Preface

Come, gather in a circle and let's have a conversation. Tell me your stories and I will tell you mine; let's talk about our experiences of becoming older. It's common for people to dodge talking or thinking about possible future care needs or to make plans for their ageing future. I wonder why? Do they see these conversations or thoughts as an admission of their physical decline and eventual death, or is the topic simply too challenging to think about?

Several people in their sixties and seventies tell me that they have no need or interest at this stage of their lives to engage in conversations about ageing well. 'What do you mean by "ageing well" and why would we need to talk about it,' they say, 'when we *are* well, still healthy, active and wonderfully comfortable and settled in our own home?'

Fair call, what is ageing well or healthy ageing? The World Health Organisation defines healthy ageing as 'the process of developing and maintaining the functional ability that enables wellbeing in older age', with wellbeing regarded as a state of being comfortable, healthy and content.[1]

However, it is now, while you *are* healthy, able to manage independently and in control of your life, that is the right time to have these discussions and make the decisions they will surely raise. That you are healthy and in control of your life may in fact be the motivation for discussion; deciding now what healthy ageing means to you and how to achieve it gives you the time to think and talk, and make informed decisions.

We are living longer and as we age there will be changes to our physical, mental and emotional health and this, over time, will lead to a natural decline in our functional and performance capacity. The 'doing things' and 'engaging in' activities will become more difficult. There are many factors, such as gender, culture, disability, finances, and our environment and lifestyle that influence how we age.

You see, for many years working within my local Community Health Services as an occupational therapist I have witnessed that, as we age and become frailer, living well at home changes and can become more challenging. By having conversations with clients 65 years and above, and providing assessments and therapeutic intervention in the client's own home, I have gained great insights into the challenges and opportunities of living safely and independently at home as you get older and possibly frailer.

The reason it's important to take the time and effort to make these plans for the future is so we can be in charge of our own futures and can plan for ageing well. We can't avoid getting older so we want to age as well as we can to make the most of our later years. By making these decisions when we are well, we relieve those left behind of a huge burden.

When I ask clients and older friends about their future goals around ageing well, most will say their wish is to live and die in their own home. Without exception they are adamant that they do not want to 'end up in a nursing home', with some stating that having to live in a nursing home in their final years is their 'greatest fear'. Experience tells me that not everyone succeeds in their aim to live to the end of their life and die in their own home. There comes a time as we get older when we will be confronted by our decline in physical and mental health and capabilities, or we experience a fall or physical crisis that leads to hospital admission. Some of these traumatic declines may well see people eventually moving into residential aged care facilities. In a crisis decisions are made rapidly, and if it is deemed that you are no longer able to live safely and independently in your own home, you will find yourself admitted into residential care. Sadly, some people end up in residential care well before they need to be there. This scenario could play out if your home environment is assessed by a health professional such as an occupational therapist to be unsafe or unsuitable to return to, or—even more likely—if there is no available care support from family, friends, neighbours, or a government care package for you to live safely and independently in your own home.

As I have reached my mid-sixties, thoughts about ageing are passing more frequently through my mind. Seeing the plight of some of my clients, and knowing the widespread wish to continue to live safely and independently at home, I wonder what we can and must do to achieve this? What enables us to direct our own living and dying?

I know that ageing well involves being positive, doing all in our power and ability to eat well, and to remain physically active, socially connected, and healthy.

But—can we do more, can YOU do more? I believe the key to ageing well into the future is the willingness to reflect on life, to learn, and to take on the challenge and the responsibility to make plans. We need to prepare for and manage the age-related changes we undergo and do this with a healthy dose of courage; it is not all about doom and gloom! To age well requires a positive and open mind and an open, loving heart.

The stories told by my clients, my ageing friends and the participants who engage in the conversation series I host have inspired me to write this book with the aim to support and engage many more people who wish to age well. This book is by people for people. I am by no means an expert on the topic, nor will I fill these pages with expert advice or surveys of people's opinions. It is my intention to present information about a topic, share stories of people's lived experience and, with this, turn the focus to you. You are the expert on your life, you have direct knowledge of and wishes for your ageing journey, and therefore you are best placed to decide what you need.

These conversations were co-designed by people like you who informed themselves, shared their experiences and supported each other. By participating and reflecting individually and together with others on the big questions and concerns around ageing well, you form a bond and build trust together. Through engaging and empowering others, we can initiate and build a supportive network that will not only be of benefit to the people engaged in the conversation but also our families, friends, communities, and our governments and possible future service providers.

This book, with its relevant conversation topics, is for people like you who are moving into and through the later stages of life and who wish to prepare themselves by making informed decisions based on values and facts about 'ageing well at home'.

These conversations are to support you to have a voice and ability to make choices about growing old at home. Make the most of this time while you are in good health to make choices for your future. This will help you to retain as active a life as possible in later years and help you to live life to the fullest in the future.

I set before you a task, a journey of a kind. The only requirement is the willingness to honestly—on your own or, better still, together with others—take time to reflect on life. This will help you to identify personal attitudes about ageing, it will highlight the opportunities and the challenges of ageing well, and it will give you a voice and ability to make choices about positively planning for your next phase of life: that of growing old at home. You will use the knowledge and experiences gained throughout your life to get organised and ready to take responsibility for the future stages of your life.

You and I do this with a dose of reality and by courageously re-examining and rediscovering what is important to us as we age. This stage of our lives offers us further unique opportunities to work out who we have become, where we belong, what realities we need to face as we get older. We explore what and who we care about, where and how we would like to live, and what we could and may need to consider as we age and, eventually, die.

This book will not provide you with all the answers, it is an invitation and an encouragement for you to use your imagination, and to consider and reflect on ageing well with meaning and purpose into the future. In whichever way you decide to use this book, I urge you to purchase a journal or notebook and write as you read. Consider sharing this book with others; your friends, peers or members of groups and clubs you belong to. Meet in turn at someone's house, or a local café or community centre, and undertake this journey together. Engage in the artistic activities that are provided in each chapter; answer the questions honestly and be willing to consider the 'what's next'. Your reactions will form and inform the conversations you have with others, your spouse/partner, children, family and friends, and assist you to make the best possible choices for your journey of ageing well.

I'll be stimulating your thoughts with ideas and extracts from my reading and from various websites. There are many people who do not have access at home to computers or the internet but you need not miss out. Public libraries and community centres offer internet access, and perhaps a family member or friend could assist. One of the advantages of sharing these conversations with friends is that you can share resources as well.

Having these conversations and making decisions on ageing well is not only for your own benefit, but it is also a way of caring for your children and those you'll leave behind when you die, or who will be in charge when you can no longer make your own decisions. Your planning now will take a huge burden off their shoulders at a time of grief.

Preparing for ageing is so important. As my good friend, a geriatrician, said to me: 'Those who do it successfully generally don't need my intervention!'

We are facing the yet unknown. Keep an open mind, explore the possibilities and take on the responsibilities. May this book stimulate you to be true to yourself, to be pro-active about ageing well; may it empower you to make choices and encourage you to live *your* life!

Introduction

Ageing is not a problem or a disease—Ageing is living!

According to the Australian Institute of Health and Welfare (AIHW), Australia's older population of people aged 65 years and over was 3.8 million in 2017, and is projected to more than double by 2057. Also expected is an increase in the number of people who will live to the age of 100 and beyond.[2]

How do we prepare ourselves for this 'getting older' phase of our lives? What does 'getting older' even mean to us individually? In 2019, I reduced my work as an occupational therapist in the community and engaged initially as a volunteer and later as a consultant with the Australian Centre for Social Innovation (TACSI). The Centre worked alongside the South Australian Health Department on projects that support ageing well, a matter I am deeply passionate about. Older Australians were asked their views on ageing and what, in their opinion, is important to support ageing well now and into the future. Ageing can mean many things to many people but after TACSI interviewed more than 1500 older South Australians several strong key themes emerged: these were consolidated into four themes that were titled 'No place like home', 'Meaningful connections', 'Money matters' and 'Navigating change'.[3]

This resonates with numerous other studies conducted which highlight that Australians have a desire to live out their days in their own home and community.[4] *The Conversation* published an article in 2020 titled 'Ageing in neighbourhood: what seniors want instead of retirement villages and how to achieve it'.[5] This article highlights people's preferences to stay in their own homes and communities instead of moving to a retirement or lifestyle village or into residential care.

Ageing at home is what is termed 'ageing in place'. It has various definitions and it is a term widely used in the aged care industry, ageing policy and in research. I am asking you to pause for a moment and think about what you understand by the phrase, and what ageing in place would mean to you?

In broad terms, ageing in place means that, as people get older, they remain living in their own home and community, safely and independently, for as long as they wish and are able. Ageing in place is a choice; it is staying in your own home, even when there is an increased risk of illness or reduced ability such as a decline in health, physical mobility or mental capacity. However, the choice of ageing in place has a responsibility attached. As you get older and start to notice a decline in health, as change is inevitable, it is important to start planning for the changes that will happen as you age, and your body and capabilities change. When we talk about supporting people to age in place, we include things like being able to ask for services and support you may need over time and as your needs change. Ageing in place is about keeping control over your own life and being flexible enough to make your own lifestyle choices. Most Australians prefer, and are choosing, to age in place and, for we older Australians, this is interrelated with keeping our independence and staying in control of our own lives, in our familiar environment, neighbourhood and local community.

However, it has also been found that most people are unprepared and reluctant to make plans for their future.[6] Fear of change also plays a part in considering change. Most have not discussed their wants and needs with anyone when it comes to making future care decisions. By not making plans we could find ourselves, when a crisis happens, making

INTRODUCTION

decisions quickly with limited information—or worse, having decisions made for us—and end up being where we do not want to be.

We, all of us, need to be aware of all the changes which are part of becoming older and we need to be active in making plans and managing these age-related changes. Not only for us 'older' adults but also for us all as an Australian community and society, for ageing affects us all, and we all age every day. This knowledge of and data about our ageing population is essential for our policy makers regarding housing, care needs and health costs, aged-based facilities and support services. Increasing numbers of us want to, and will be, with available and supportive care if need be, 'ageing in place'.

Age does not play a role in forward planning; it is not that when you turn 65 or 70 you must start thinking about your ageing future – you can do it at any stage of your life. It could be that the people in your immediate environment, your children, neighbours or friends, or community organisations with whom you are in contact are the ones who encourage you to think about this next phase of your life. Most often it is major life changes that compel us to make changes in our living situation, such as children leaving home, birth of grandchildren, retirement or retrenchment and associated loss of income, illness and/or disability, or death of a spouse or loved one.

We, this coming generation of older people, will be ageing differently than our parents aged twenty or thirty years ago. We have seen a change in the role of policy makers, funding bodies and service providers, and as older people we are now encouraged to do more for ourselves. The Covid-19 pandemic and its associated national debt will have profound effects into the future that we cannot yet clearly see. How can you and will you live the life you want to live within the constraints of your own lived situation? What would you like, what do you need and what must you do to prepare to age well?

Most of us have a desire to keep our vitality, remain socially well connected and to remain active within our own home and community.

And for most of us there is also a wish to live a life that has meaning, where there is a purpose and a sense that we each matter.

People who prepare for their ageing future consider questions such as: What makes me happy? Where can I still contribute? What challenges do I still want to undertake? Who or what does and will still inspire me? How can I live this next phase of my life? The answers to these questions will be different for each of us. However, wouldn't it be wonderful to have a conversation with others about what keeps you going and what keeps you 'alive'? In the sharing of our stories and the listening to others, we support each other to make sense of what is happening and help us prepare.

In partnership with TACSI, I co-designed a conversation series with and for older adults, which was facilitated on numerous occasions in local communities, either in a small group or a circle of 12 to 15 people. Engaging in-person has huge benefits as it enables each person to share understandings and feelings around ageing and learn what a variety of other people are doing.

The Covid pandemic that began in 2020 forced us all to re-consider face-to-face engagement and has made many people think differently about the future. I am no different, and I have therefore decided to write down my experiences and make the learnings and stories available in a book. This book you are holding now will enable many more people to engage in dialogue with others. During a pandemic it is even more prudent to consider our ageing future, to engage in community and to look out for one another. We need to ensure that as a community we take care of ourselves, each other, and other members, young and old, within our society!

While writing, I engaged with several people aged 65 years and above in person, via phone, email, or other digital interaction groups and several of them kindly agreed to have their 'lived' story included in this book. I've changed their names for privacy. Let's start with Pascal ...

INTRODUCTION

Pascal is 72 years old, married with four adult children, and stated that he was 'motivated to contribute' as a main reason to engage in the conversations. For him, ageing well means staying 'outward focused', by which he means not just focusing on oneself but considering what he can do to support others within his family, neighbourhood and community. Pascal has seen friends deteriorate after retirement by being too self-attentive, and he has little respect for some baby boomers who, having enjoyed a 'pretty lucky' existence, now see no need to give to community even though they have all the time in the world. While he still works on a part-time basis Pascal is also involved as a volunteer in various organisations at a community level and he has a high respect for volunteers and activists.

Pascal is just one of the generous and interesting people I met while carrying out my conversations. As you read the book you will meet more of these thoughtful people.

Let me now introduce you to the ten conversation starters that make up the book. Each topic will have some general information that is interspersed and highlighted with individual stories. You will be encouraged to undertake some activities including reflective journaling and going on fact-finding missions. These exploratory journeys help you get a sense of the living future you want to create, who are the people, what and where is the information, and where are the places of most potential that could inform and teach you most about the future and how to make ageing work for you. Use these topics and engage in formal or informal chats, discussions, heart to hearts, and exchanges of ideas with others: your family and friends, your health and medical advisors, groups that you belong to in the community, local councils and government organisations. These conversations are all about how YOU can age well at home in your community.

There is no need to read this book in the order in which the conversation themes are presented. The book is written so that you can pick the theme that is relevant or that takes your interest on any given day—dip in and out as you please. The intention is that you think and reflect on what is offered. Take time to mull things over and consider how they are relevant to your life. This book will not provide you with all the answers as the answers are different for each one of us. What it will do is give you plenty to think about and resources where you can find more information.

Before you read further, consider the following questions about your life now and how you see your ageing future. Use your notebook to record your thoughts and answers, and highlight those issues you want to come back to:

- What or who motivated you to buy or read this book?
- What, for you, is aging well?
- What are the issues you consider when thinking about ageing well?
- What is important for you regarding ageing well in your community?
- What do you hope to get out of this book and possible conversations with others?
- What is your current lifestyle? Do you see it remaining much the same as you age?
- What do you expect your future ageing years to look like? Is it what you would hope for?

Topics of conversation

1. **Home, Belonging and Community** explores our sense of place. This means exploring our external place—where we live, our home and community—as well as our 'inner' feelings of where we really belong.
2. **The Realities of Ageing** raises awareness of our physical, psychological, emotional, and social wellbeing and helps us plan for ageing well.

3. **Ageism:** What is it, how does it affect us and how do we respond to it? How do we contribute to or engage in ageism? And how can we work to reverse it?
4. **Money Matters** encourages us to work out the finances we need to age well. Money does matter so it is important to consider what expenses we may have as we age and how we can manage the funds, however meagre, we will have access to.
5. **Care and Care Support** contrasts care at home, care in an institution and care support within community. Ageing in place means exploring support and care options in advance for future changes so we are prepared when care is needed.
6. **The Importance of Social Connection** makes the case that social connections are especially important for us to age well. This topic inspires us to look at our social connections and the significance they have in our lives as we age.
7. **Alternative Housing Options** describes some alternative housing options for older people and encourages us to consider the most suitable housing options for our ageing future. Is there a case for downsizing or 'right-sizing' your home as you grow older? What is available for those who don't own their own home?
8. **Living with Meaning and Purpose** inspires us to age well. We all matter, live with meaning, deal with fear, and come to terms with our mortality. Do you know or have a sense that your life matters? Is there a form of spirituality that is important to you?
9. **Planning for End of Life** invites you to consider your wishes as you may become frailer and more dependent, about how to die a 'good death' and what a 'good death' looks like to you. It also suggests you consider formalising your wishes by preparing an advance care directive, so that you wishes cannot be overridden.
10. **Planning for your Funeral:** We plan for births, special occasions and weddings, why not funerals? How would you like to celebrate your life and what sort of occasion would you want your funeral

to be? What do you want done with your body? What is your budget?

The last two chapters of the book, **Courage to Change** and **On Your Way**, encourage you to act on the thoughts and decisions you've made as you have worked through and discussed the ten topics. The first encourages us to cope with change and to create meaning from the challenges of ageing. We explore courage and consider creative solutions and the options of taking some risks. The second, our final chapter, will help you take that next step to ageing well.

To age well requires us to have an open mind, to be positive, to remain active, informed and socially connected, to stay as healthy as we can, and to be willing and able to manage changes within what our individual expectations are.

This talking and planning about ageing well is challenging work. You may at times feel uncomfortable and overwhelmed, and have a wish to stop the thinking, the conversations and the decision making. On those occasions, stop a moment to take stock and give your mind a rest. Take your time, but you must get back to this work and keep moving forward. We derive our value from what we contribute.

Note: Make sure you stay emotionally well and seek professional support if it becomes all too challenging.

Introduction

I am not old

I am not old, she said,
I am rare.

I am the standing ovation
at the end of the play.

I am the retrospective
of my life
as art.

I am the hours
connected like dots
into good sense.

I am the fullness
of existing.

You think I am waiting to die
But I am waiting to be found.

I am a treasure,
I am a map,
these wrinkles are
imprints of my journey.

Ask me
anything.

– Samantha Reynolds, *Musing on Life*, www.bentlily.com

CHAPTER 1

Home, Belonging and Community

A place where we live matters but more importantly it needs to be 'home', a place where we feel we belong.
— Hugh Mackay, The Art of Belonging

This first chapter explores our sense of place, our external place. I ask you to 'recce' your home and community as well as your inner feelings of where you really belong. You might need to start by asking yourself what it means to belong.

Our home situates in our community. Our community is not just a geographical location on a map or in a postcode area. Community or neighbourhood is a living organism with integrated relationships between people, neighbours, organisations and businesses, and groups. We know when we are there, we feel it, 'this is the place where I need to be'.

Merily, 73, has been living with her partner in the same house for the last 34 years, and that house is strongly connected to her sense of home, of belonging.

'Home is the centre of our family, a place from which we leave and to which we return. Home is our safe place where friends feel comfortable to come visit and share meals. The sharing of food has always played an important role in our home as it helps to create a contented and welcoming ambiance. It is a place where we welcome home our children and grandchildren for a catch-up and conversation and they know they can usually count on us for a good feed! Their visits illuminate the day and warm the heart. The physical part of 'home' is using my own kitchen utensils, my pretty crockery each with a memory of being collected, and lots of flowers. My own bedroom with my red bed, my paintings covering the walls, my lamp to read my artbooks and my big windows framing my garden.'

This topic of home and belonging fascinates me, and it has played a role in my life for a really long time. I cannot remember the number of times that, when I first meet someone new, they ask me: 'Where are you from?' It seems such a simple question, but what does it really mean? Where do I live? Where have I lived? Where was I born? In my case, it is likely that my accent, still perceptible even after living in Australia for more than 40 years, gives me away. I often turn the question into a guessing game and pose a counter question: 'Have a guess', I would say, 'where do you think I come from?' Particularly when meeting a client for the first time, this brief, getting-to-know-you question and answer conversation helps to build initial rapport and trust.

I was born in the Netherlands and home was a small dairy village north of Amsterdam. It was home, I felt safe, and I belonged there. As child I was unable to have 'sleep overs' at my cousins' place as they were living in another village about 10 kilometres away. I suffered from homesickness which meant I didn't thrive when away from home for even a couple of days. As a young adult studying nursing in a hospital setting approximately 60 kilometres from home, I managed well but interestingly, when my days off came around, I would catch the earliest train home. My parents were most amazed when I announced at the age of 21 that I would follow the love of my life to Australia! Australia became home but even here there have been some interesting journeys and a number of different places we have called home. Within Australia we have lived in four different states and, for me, the most difficult move of my life was from Sydney, New South Wales, to the Adelaide Hills in South Australia. Sydney, where we had lived and worked for 16 years, where our children were born and where we had a supportive circle of friends, where we felt part of our local and school communities, had become home to us, and leaving that place initially left me with a deep sense of loss.

Now, as I get older, this question of 'Where is home for you?' is still relevant. Home and belonging still play a role in my thinking and I have realised, for several years now, that yes, Australia is very much home for me and yes, a part of me still belongs in the Netherlands. When I visit, and particularly when I walk and cycle those flat lands with their canals and big wide-open skies, I have a great sense of joy and contentment.

Pascal expresses that deep inner feeling of belonging in the connection and relationship with his wife Petra, his family and his sense of spirituality: 'The family is far and away my locus of stability. I belong deeply when with Petra and the children.' Pascal's time of greatest non-belonging was when he was in Canada for five years studying for his PhD, and he expresses that he suffered a deep feeling of loneliness and a sense of loss about where he wanted to be. It was at that time that Pascal had an experience that, since then, he calls his anchor point.

'I was sitting in an armchair reading peacefully alone one evening, a pleasant lamp lending a pleasant glow. I was calm and at peace. Then out of the blue, over my left shoulder, came a voice: 'Don't worry, everything will be all right.' I've had other revelatory moments, but they've been flashes of intuitive insight. I have also prayed over the years in an attempt to experience a closeness with God. But this moment involved a voice from outside me and without any attempt on my part. Anyway, you could say that I have as a religious person a sense of being surrounded by God's love and care. And that is an important, stabilising sense of belonging.'

Where do *you* belong, where and what is home for you? It is the most important place in our lives. When our friends visit we want them to feel welcomed and comfortable so we might ask them to 'make themselves at home'. That sense of feeling at home promotes our physical and mental health and, by the same token, not having a home increases our risk of stress. It appears that home and belonging have four characteristics, which are:

1. A sanctuary, a place you feel safe, can be yourself and seclude yourself
2. A feeling of control, where you can influence the things that happen
3. A sense of connection and belonging, and
4. A sense of identity, that you are someone of consequence within your family and circle.

If all these qualities are present you experience a warm fuzzy feeling of 'being at home'.[7]

Settle back and relax into some reflective thinking about what home and belonging mean to you. Consider the following reflective questions and write your thoughts in your notebook.

- Where in the world do you belong?
- What gives you that sense of belonging?
- What are the aspects of place that make it 'home' for you?
- What is your background story and what are your experiences around home and belonging?

If you are at home, look around you; if not, use your memory. Ask yourself: What is it about this place that makes it home? I encourage you to find a small object that is part of making your house a home. Place it next to you or picture it in your mind's eye, and write about it in your notebook: how is this part of making your house a home?

HOME, BELONGING AND COMMUNITY

Merily said that she had not considered home and belonging before our conversation, but now sees how much she had taken it for granted. She said:

> 'If my partner died and I was left on my own, I would consider moving. I would not rush this, what would be a major change, but living in this house with all its strong memories would, I believe, exaggerate the loneliness without having the emotional support from my closest friend as well as his physical input in enabling [me] to maintain this large house and garden.'

Merily is willing to move to a new house, but she would like to remain close to her circle of family and friends, and says of any potential move: 'it is paramount that it is a place where you feel safe'.

In *Claiming Your Place at the Fire*, a book describing a new model of vital ageing for people moving through the second half of their lives, authors Leider and Shapiro speak about 'the power of place' and how changes in relationships, work and health naturally hasten the need for us to reconsider our sense of place as we age.[8]

Next door to my home in the Adelaide Hills is a retirement village and we are friendly with several people who live there. They are our neighbours and form part of our local community. Anne, one of the residents, is in her mid-nineties; she moved into the village around four years ago. Anne is not able to settle, she is not happy living there, she misses her old home and her community, her familiar environment. Anne lived in a small rural village approximately 75 kilometres away from where she is now. The southern Adelaide Hills, in her old home within her known community, is where Anne feels she belongs. As she got older and needed more support her family members suggested Anne move closer to where her daughter lives so her daughter could visit more regularly and have less difficulty taking Anne to her medical appointments. Anne understood this and, not wanting to be an extra burden, agreed to move. However, she feels lonely and is simply not 'at home' in her home in this retirement village, 'living with all old people', as Anne puts it. She has the most wonderful expressions and one of them is: 'you should not move old trees as they often fail to thrive in new surroundings'. Anne's comments echo Leider and Shapiro's: 'Just as no tree can grow tall unless it is firmly rooted in the soil, so we, too, cannot continue to flourish unless we have set down roots in the place we really belong'.[9]

Anne enjoyed living in the southern Hills and had a strong sense of belonging there and, while she was fit and healthy, did not consider her future ageing or possible need for extra support. It is this stage of our lives, between 60 and 75 years of age and while many of us are still in good health, that provides a unique opportunity for exploring what is next in life. In this period, we may have the opportunity to choose how and where we live, how and with whom we like to engage, and where we hope to age in place. If only we could have a crystal ball—it would help us to know if we could remain living in our own home till the end of our days or if we indeed might need to consider moving to a more suitable home or location. But mightn't knowing everything in advance ruin some delightful surprises too?

According to Pascal, it is all related to staying outward focussed and showing resilience.

> 'I am fascinated by the options which my generation are looking at regarding where they live as they age. Friends have 'downsized', swapped a 5-bedroom home in Colonel Light Gardens [suburban Adelaide] for a same-sized home just outside Victor Harbor [seaside town south of Adelaide]; we have thought of doing the granny flat thing. And so on. Conversely, climate change anxiety is driving our three daughters—all interstate for a decade or more—to want to come back to be near their parents. Which means that we ourselves are staying open to the idea of living where we are in Belair [outer suburban Adelaide]—a home which managed to bring up a family of four plus us—as the hub. Not that long ago it was a simple exercise of downsizing.'

For now, Pascal and his wife Petra are staying put while remaining realistic, and aware and open minded about future options.

When you think about wanting to age in your own home, I am curious to know how you see your ageing scenario. What are your real-life experiences, of your parents, siblings or friends? Delia's parents Daisy and Archie, whose story you will read about in Chapter Five, had every intention to age in place. The couple were both in fair health, active, engaged in community and fiercely independent with a preference to overlook their ageing future. Regrettably, they had not considered the 'what ifs' for the future, such as their house on a large, steeply sloping hill and a big, high-maintenance garden, the internal layout of the house dated and not meeting their ageing needs, and their dependence on a car and driver's license as they lived a short distance from local services and shops. 'We are fine in our home', they kept saying—until the wheels fell off and events occurred that Daisy and Archie had not anticipated.

For Pascal, ageing in place means first and foremost ageing as a resilient self. Limited finances play a role. Pascal and Petra were a single income family for most of their child-rearing life, and with two of their four children living with significant and ongoing health issues, it took all Petra's time and energies to manage. Says Pascal,

> 'We're not particularly well off and we still have a mortgage. This means we are not going into older age with much superannuation or large assets and therefore won't be able to choose a wonderful retirement village. Our fiscal circumstances might not be brilliant but for us the inner and family lives are more important.'

Pascal is not sure what the future will bring and finds it, for now, too challenging to consider.

Times are changing, we say, what was once is different now. Historically, what do you believe ageing in place meant?

When the health of my grandmother-in-law, Grandma Lee, declined when she was nearly 90 and became frailer and needed more support, she discussed in collaboration with her children how they could manage. Living on her own was no longer a safe option and unfortunately in the small rural township where she lived there were few care services available. With her children, Grandma Lee decided that she would live in turn with each of her four children for a period of 3 months. For the family, and especially Grandma Lee, this worked well; she was loved and respected by all her children, children-in-law and grandchildren, and she felt at home with each family. Grandma Lee lived in turn with her children over a period of two years between 1979 and early 1981, when she died.

My parents-in-law's story is a bit different. They lived on a 20-acre property at the edge of a large rural city. When they were in their late seventies and experiencing declining health, we raised the question of how they saw their ageing future. My father-in-law suffered from chronic airway disease and needed extra support. Together he and Mum were no longer able to manage the care and maintenance of a large house and twenty acres of land. Each of their five children had asked them how they were managing and if they had considered downsizing. When we spoke with them, we asked what they had considered. Living independently was still important to them as was remaining within their region and their community. That was familiar, there they volunteered, engaged in church and community activities, and met with their circle of friends.

Of their five children only two lived in the same rural town, the other three at a large distance or interstate. Mum had always expressed her wish that if Dad were to die before her and she was no longer able to live in her own home (ageing in place), she would, like her mother in her final years, wish to live in turn with each of her five children. Yet here was the dilemma. When Mum's mother, Grandma Lee, lived in turn with each of her children it was a very different time. Each of Grandma's daughters or daughters-in-law (she had two of each) were stay-at-home women and therefore seen to have more capacity to provide care for Grandma. This was quite different to the time after Dad had died and Mum lived on her own. None of her children were able to have Mum stay for an extended period. Her daughter and her four daughters-in-law were either in business, working or studying. Times had changed and providing care for a live-in elderly parent was not an easy option. My husband was one of Mum's children who lived interstate, we both worked and our children were teenagers going to school or university. We felt that we could not provide Mum with the care, support, social interaction and meaningful activity she needed and deserved.

In the end one of Mum's granddaughters, who was studying at the local university, went to live with her. This worked very well for both, it provided Mum with a live-in support person and gave her life new meaning. As a widow, and now with her granddaughter living in, Mum's tasks were cooking meals, doing the laundry, and all other activities she was still able to manage. When she needed help her granddaughter was there to lend a hand. They were great companions together and looked out for one another. When her granddaughter graduated she found a job a long way away and moved out. It was clear that Mum missed the companionship and support very much, especially the companionship. Although she had enormous support and assistance from her sons and families who lived nearby, it was not the same as sharing a house with another person. Mum did experience loneliness in the final stage of her life.

These two ageing stories, of Grandma Lee and, more than thirty years later, of Mum, highlight the different ageing scenarios each experienced. The ensuing 35 years had brought many changes. Accordingly, what does 'ageing in place' mean today, and how will it be for me as I get older and need more support or even care?

So, consider for a moment: What is your present living and ageing scenario? How do you see your future? How will you react as your sphere of ability tightens? Is a change needed? What choices can you make to roll with the changes rather than fight them? Are you currently able to make the required decisions? Make a few notes in your journal. Leider and Shapiro suggest that our 'challenge is to discover the basis on which to choose to move or stay, cling to or renew'.[10] We tend to ignore the issue or freeze when it all gets too hard or when we are challenged—which is unlikely the most appropriate or helpful response. I believe that, deep within, you know, you have a sense of what is required to age well in your own home. It takes courage to acknowledge a required relocation or home modifications, it needs imagination and courage to consider the options and discuss them with loved ones. Ageing in place, at home, within your community, does mean you take on the responsibility to plan and make decisions for any future changes.

Further on in this book, when we discuss housing, I will tell you more about how the need to belong had my husband and I become village builders, and we are now turning the nearly two-acre piece of land on which our house is built into a co-housing community. To age in place, we need to have access to a 'good home within a supportive community' as that is most important to a sense of belonging and ageing well! As Leider and Shapiro write:

> A real sense of belonging to a place involves more than just physical comfort. A sense that we are seen by others, that our contributions matter, that we are making a difference and touching people's lives plays an even more vital role in helping us to feel like we're where in the world we belong.[11]

Home is where the heart is

Reflect on the following questions and jot down some answers or responses:

1. What sort of physical environment helps you to feel most at home?
2. What medical and social services are essential to your sense of safety and place?

3. What cultural activities do you need in the place you call home? Do you enjoy movies, theatre or music? Do you prefer to do these alone or with company?
4. What opportunities are available for you to engage in clubs, groups or organisations within your community? Why are/aren't you involved in these activities?
5. What opportunities are available for you to express your calling through work or volunteering in this community?
6. How often do you drive to do errands or other activities? How much time does this take? What other transport options are there?
7. How important is it for you to be living near your family?
8. How important are your neighbours? How well do you know them?
9. How often do you visit friends who are within walking distance?
10. What are the day-to-day activities that you pursue now? How much time do they take and which ones do you prefer? Do you keep physically active?
11. For activities such as cooking and eating, do you enjoy doing these alone or do you prefer company?
12. Do you enjoy gardening? Do you have an interest in growing your own food, or do you garden for the enjoyment of growing things? Do you like to garden with a friend or alone?
13. Would you rather relax outside, alone, or with company? Do you like to go for walks, cycle or an exercise class?
14. How often do you have phone conversations with distant friends and family?
15. Is watching TV a norm in your life? How often do you watch TV?
16. Do you like listening to radio or podcasts, or reading blogs?
17. Do you like to read? And if you do, do you like discussing what you read with others?

18. Do you enjoy having guests in your home? Do you enjoy hosting friends or family? Would you rather visit a friend in their house?
19. Are pets an important part of your life?[12]

Artistic Activity

Before you read on, I encourage you to do an artistic activity. You may like to invite a few friends and do this activity together so you can discuss it. Get old magazines, a collection of photographs, a large sheet of paper, some colour pencils, scissors and glue and create a collage representing what the aspects of home and belonging are for you. Alternatively, write a story or a poem about what gives you a sense of place.

CHAPTER 2

The Realities of Ageing

The reality of getting older is that our bodies age and that nothing will stop this ageing process. There will be ever-increasing factors that will influence illness, cause organ failure or memory loss, wrinkle our skin, grey our hair, and place limitations on our sight, hearing, smell, taste, touch, mobility and our activities of daily living. The reality is that ageing will change all of us, no matter how fit we are and how much we take care of our bodies with good nutrition, exercise, mental stimulation and maintaining a positive outlook on life. Ageing is a process and—apparently—we reach our physical peak at mid-twenties and start to get 'old' from early adulthood; eventually, as we age into older age, we become frailer physically and mentally. Victoria's Department of Health describes frailty as 'a multidimensional geriatric syndrome characterised by a decline of physical and cognitive reserves that lead to increased vulnerability'.[13]

It is this increase in frailty and infirmity that many older people are afraid of. We cannot stop ageing, we cannot fix it, and inevitably getting older means a decline in health. As a result of improvements in health care, living conditions, health care education, income, and better control of infectious diseases we are now living longer than our ancestors and, as part of living longer, we are more likely to die from age-related or lifestyle diseases such as cardio-vascular diseases, neurodegenerative diseases, and cancer. We cannot stop ageing, but we *can* do our best to keep physically, psychologically and emotionally healthy, by taking action, such as eating a healthy diet and regular physical and mental exercises, to limit lifestyle related diseases.

Research tells us that vitality is part genes, part environment and part mindset and zest for life.[14] Each person experiences the 'getting older' bit in a different form, which could be a negative or a positive experience. Merily, at 72, is experiencing increased health problems. She was diagnosed with cancer five years ago.

> 'I have always had extraordinary energy and good health and it is difficult to know if it is age or this chronic condition I have that is causing a drop-off in energy and inability to work as productively as I would wish. I suspect it is both and am unhappy with this. Mentally I have had to lower my expectations on what I can do and plan for. It seems downhill in what I can achieve and the idea of being so frail as to lose my independence is a fate worse than death for me! I feel comforted that I will probably die of my condition before that happens.'

Pascal, on the other hand, finds himself at 72 in robust health, but he says:

> 'I'm not keeping my body up as the vital housing for my mind and spirit. I work out with two mates on Saturday mornings. Otherwise, I hardly get any exercise beyond a bit of gardening. In contrast, our diet is excellent – largely vegetarian, low in fats and sugars, with homemade sourdough bread and an endless supply of home-brewed kombucha and kefir water. This is driven by Petra who is determined that both of us will have good gut health and strong immune systems. Left to myself, well…!'

Pascal goes on to say that he is increasingly conscious that life expectancy is becoming more of a lottery and mentioned feeling blessed to have a life far richer than he had imagined as a teenager: 'My father died at 58, so having lived well beyond that seems a bonus.'

Pascal reflected deeply on the questions around his feelings about ageing and what it means to him. He shared with me how his life story this far influences and colours his attitude to ageing. Together with Petra, his life partner, they have been a team throughout married life. It has been a relationship based on shared values, overlapping interests, spirituality, the nurturing of their children and a commitment to community. Raising their children brought its challenges with two of their four children having significant and ongoing chronic health problems, plus the impact of the constant health crises on their other two children. As Pascal says, supporting and guiding these four children has been a mammoth and never-ending task—of which 80 per cent fell to Petra. Regarding ageing, Pascal mentions having only one overarching goal:

> 'to stay alive as long as I can for the sake of Petra, the children and the grandchildren. When our eldest was born the words of St Paul came to mind: 'I am no longer my own master. I have been bought and sold.' Petra and I have often described ourselves as chief shareholders of the 'Family Inc'. I want to continue being there for them all for their sakes, not mine. That is mainly emotional. I did not know my grandparents really, only one of whom was a hazy memory and a disengaged and, I learned later, alcoholic old woman. I want my two grandchildren and any later grandchildren all to be at least ten before I go. I want them all to have rich and happy memories of a fun, lively and engaged grandpa!'

Getting older could mean a natural and gradually advancing process without any significant aspects of declining or ill health. Older age is a period in which you may reflect on life and acknowledge some wisdom gained, a time of more freedom, new interests and less responsibilities. For several of us, it can also be a stage in life associated with increased health problems and concerns, and a period of loss and change. This may depend on which age or stage of ageing you are at. The 'younger' older person may experience excellent health with an ability to explore new-gained freedom and interests, while the 'older' older person may experience increasing problems with health and wellbeing.

Ageing can be step-by-step, just like life itself, or it can be a sudden reality, as Jackie experienced. A healthy and active 67-year-old, Jackie went on a holiday to Tasmania three years ago. It was there that she had a fall.

> 'I injured myself when I flew backwards whilst I slid on a somewhat slippery wet deck. Landing on my back, I broke a vertebra in my spine. After months of very painful, slow, and limited movement I was lucky enough to emerge upright with full mobility in all my limbs. The lengthy rehabilitation gave me time to think, and the fall gave me the shock treatment I needed to consider my long-term future with a previously denied clarity.'

As Jackie shared with me, she had not planned this fall—accidents happen—but on reflection she admitted to a slowing down of her reflexes, a slight deterioration in her balance and a dizziness when she turned too quickly. 'Stuff that is easily ignored and the "it won't happen to me" syndrome is a seductive option.' Jackie has no intention of having another fall but, as she said, 'I had no intention to fall in the first place!' It was a reality check for her, all of a sudden ageing and loss of mobility was not something that happens to other people: it was something that happened to her. Jackie has accepted that reality and since her fall has made many changes in her home and life to prepare for an ageing future. For instance, she fully modified her bathroom to ensure ease of access and safety, removed an internal wall to create a more spacious kitchen dining area, secured level and safe pathways to her front and back doors and created a more older-person-friendly garden with raised beds and level pathways.

The Realities of Ageing

Any of us at any time may find ourselves in need to make changes to continue living safely and comfortably in our own homes. Consider the following home modifications to make your house more ageing friendly:
- ease of access to front and back door entrances
- widening doorways or removal of walls to create ease of access and movement internally
- kitchen modifications like the height of cupboards and appliances
- bathroom modifications such as separate shower, bars beside toilet and bath
- flooring modifications to prevent slipping and tripping
- medical or safety alert systems
- assistive devices or assistive seating.

For advice you could contact the Independent Living Centre in your state or search their website.[15] And I highly recommend you seek the assessment and advice of an occupational therapist and physiotherapist if having falls is a high risk factor.

Ageing happens and it cannot be postponed. Slowly but surely the ageing process catches up with us and we may find that the last stages can be a bit frayed. This fraying is not to be ignored but needs to be acknowledged and, as far as is possible, planned for.

Let's look at the realities of getting older: we become less mobile, our bodies stiffen up, we move more slowly, we have deterioration in our sight and hearing, we may lose our ability to drive and become less able (or less willing) to quickly adapt to new places and new situations. How are your knees, eyes, hips, feet, skin, ears, your mind and your heart? I am curious to know how these facts resonate with you. How do you experience ageing and how do you feel about ageing, what does it mean to you? Are you accepting or are you in denial? Are you worried and what would you be most worried about?

When I convene an eight or ten-week in-person conversation series with a group of 12 to 15 participants I bring out a series of cards when we get to this session and do an activity which I call 'the cards we get dealt in life' or the 'what if' cards. Each of these cards sets out a scenario. I invite people to form small groups, hand them a few cards and invite the groups to discuss the scenarios as outlined on the cards. I ask them: What would you do if you were in this situation, or could you find yourself in this situation in the future?

Here are some examples of the scenarios.

Scenario 1.

Simone, 78, and John, 81, are living on a 5-acre rural block, in an old cottage which has been built into the hillside. As they are ageing, they have not been able to keep up with all the maintenance. The pathways around the house are uneven and there are ten steps up to the front and four steps at the back leading to the veranda. The interior of the cottage is rather dated and cluttered, and it is becoming increasingly difficult, as Simone and John are getting older, for them to get in and out of the bath in which their overhead shower is located. Due to declining eyesight John is no longer able to drive. Simone suffers from peripheral neuropathy and has decreased sensation in her feet and has therefore also given up her driving.

Scenario 2.

You have recently been diagnosed with Alzheimer's disease. Your life partner died three years ago and now you are worried about your future. How will you continue to manage on your own? Your two children live interstate, and they are busy with their families and work commitments. You don't want to be a burden on your family.

Scenario 3.

After retirement you and your partner decided to sell up your home in New South Wales, buy a motorhome and travel. You are having a great time until suddenly your partner dies. You end up in a caravan park near your daughter who lives in a semi-rural location. Your daughter provides support, but she also has a full-time job. Lately you feel a bit clumsy and have had a few falls and you are getting a bit anxious. The GP sends you to a specialist and you receive the diagnosis of Parkinson's disease. Not surprisingly, with all the losses you are experiencing, you fall in a heap and wonder how to move on with life.

Scenario 4.

You have slipped in the bathroom and have broken your hip. Now what? Six months later you are still struggling as there have been complications. You have noticed that since your fall you have become a lot more anxious. Who has provided support? What do you need to consider?

Initially group members are reluctant to engage and find these scenario's farfetched and unrealistic—Jackie would have put herself in this category until she had her fall. However, each of these cards tells the story of a real-life scenario. All these scenarios were lived experiences of the numerous clients I met as an occupational therapist working within my local community. How would it be for you if you had a fall and fractured a bone, or you received a diagnosis of Alzheimer's or Parkinson's disease? You may not live in a motorhome but how would you manage this in your life as it is now and into the future?

Perception is oftentimes different from reality. Merily joined one of my first conversation circles. She is a friend, and took part because she wanted to support me in this endeavour. Although Merily engaged at a social level, there appeared to be a reluctance in engaging at a deeper, personal level to explore what it could mean for her as life changed. Merily's life is changing now that she has been living with cancer for several years. Recently, she heard that her cancer treatment is not supporting her as well as she had hoped. Together, we have regular open and honest conversations and explore the 'what if's' for the future. The 'what if' cards help you to consider matters physically, environmentally, socially and mentally and—most importantly—make plans. There is a wonderful quote by Randy Pausch in 'The Last Lecture: Really achieving your childhood dreams' where he says, 'We cannot change the cards we are dealt, just how we play the hand.'[16]

Every individual will experience the process of ageing in a different way, and this could depend on your gender, genes, culture, education, geographical location, environment and life circumstances. One of the scenarios highlighted in the cards might be your future scenario. We each experience our own journey of ageing, and what these stories and scenarios aim to do is to get us thinking about what it would mean if we were in that situation. How would we manage? What changes may we need to consider so that we continue to age well even while experiencing limitations in life? According to an interim report from the Royal Commission into Aged Care Quality and Safety it is not uncommon for older people to avoid thinking about their long-term care needs or plan for their future as they feel that this may signal their decline and eventual death.[17] It seems most people take one of two approaches: either they are confident that they will be looked after when their time comes, or they simply hope to 'die in their sleep one night' and so don't have to worry about it!

I encourage you, as I encourage myself, to *get out of denial* and accept your status quo, accept the hand you were dealt! Yes, I am somewhat stiffer in my limbs, I do wear glasses and there is some evidence of emerging cataracts in my eyes and (according to my husband) it is time for me to have a hearing check. Other than that, I am fit and healthy, and all is well in my world. Ageing happens to others, my neighbours, friends, and clients, but when looking in the mirror I know that, at 65, my physiological peak is well behind me. Interestingly, as I re-read these last few lines, I can see that by the language I use in the words 'somewhat' and 'some evidence' and 'according to others', that there *is* denial. Why would I not admit that I am stiffer in my limbs, have emerging cataracts and acknowledge that it is a good idea to get my hearing tested? Is prevention not better than cure? Ageing does play a role in my life, why else would I have even considered writing a book about ageing well? Part of me is in denial, but a larger part of me is passionately interested in ageing well. I like to make sense of what is happening to me, my clients, and my ageing family and friends. How do we experience this slowly getting older? Through working with ageing and already elderly clients and having observed and engaged with the ageing life of my mother who lived to 98, I have witnessed how ageing is experienced by many different people. It appears that needs related to life after 65 seem to be dealt with after they come up, rather than anticipated and planned for. I am a realist and know how important it is to get out of denial, reframe expectations and to start planning early. Merily is moving through her denial and is facing reality, and with this she is making plans for her future while continuing to enjoy, to the best of her ability, all life has to offer.

I urge you to have a conversation with others—but please remember to not turn your conversations into an 'organ recital' where you harp on about your aches and pain. Deal with issues at hand, make plans. Ask yourself, how can I change myself or make changes to my environment to make life better? If you maintain control over your own life, you not only ensure you don't leave a mess or a challenge for those left behind but you are also more likely to get the future you want rather than having to make do with what is thrust upon you by circumstance. Look at this planning as a positive and proactive way to enrich your own life and make the most of the years and the opportunities you have remaining. If we can appreciate these later stages of life, we will see ageing in a different light and move forward with living and enjoying our life!

How strange it is to get older

*I won't subject you
to the details,
just that I was biking
and then I wasn't.*

*It's not that my leg won't heal,
just that it will take longer.*

*"because of my age,"
the doctor said.*

*Which happened to be
on the same day
I learned that VHS tapes
were invented
the year I was born.*

*The VHS tapes
that are now extinct.*

*And now I see
what my mother meant
about how strange
it is to get older.*

*The changes suddenly speed up
as though aging is a thing
that chases.*

The Realities of Ageing

First, a leg.
Earlobes seem looser too.
Veins have popped on my hands
as though families of caterpillars
are hiding under the blanket
of my skin.

And yet, I am still as bright inside
as I have ever been,
as I will always be,
evolving and unfolding.

See my light,
I hear them clearly now,
women of my mother's age,
that chorus of fierce hearts
I will soon join.

Samantha Reynolds, *Musings on Life*, www.bentlily.com

CHAPTER 3

Ageism

United Nations report headline, March 2021: 'Ageism is a global challenge'—this report from the World Health Organisation (WHO) states that 'Ageism leads to poorer health, social isolation, earlier deaths and cost economies billions: report calls for swift action to implement anti-ageism strategies.'[18]

'Don't forget your seniors card,' says my husband as I walk out of the house to shop at our local fruit and veg market, 'remember it is seniors' discount day! You will need it as they won't believe you are over 60!' He is a charmer, that husband of mine (despite gently mentioning hearing checks!). When I get to the check-out and offer my seniors card the check-out operator says, 'Oh, no need, I've entered the discount already.' She must have looked at my greying hair and wrinkled face and decided I was 'old'. I had a chuckle, still feeling young but by a younger generation seen as old. I made light of it, but even this incident, my husband's retort, my own sense of feeling flattered, and the shop assistants reply, I recognise as subtle forms of ageism. The above-mentioned WHO report states that 'every second person in the world is believed to hold ageist attitudes'![19] Read that again—yes, every second person! This shocked me and, on honest reflection, I realise that figure includes me. I have on occasions subtly or overtly in my thinking, engagement or behaviour acted with an ageist attitude. Not good and it must change. Ageism has indeed seeped into our societies. As Jane Mussared, former CEO of COTA SA, states: 'We need to own up to ageism – our own and that of our community. It limits us, talks us into uncertain inevitabilities, kills our imagination and suggests we already know what so-called ageing well is and looks like.'[20]

Ageism is discrimination based on age and it can affect every one of us, at any age. It is growing within our society and, although it is discrimination against any age group, ageism is more prevalent as a discrimination against older people, as negative stereotyping of older adults.

I'm going to quote the entire opening paragraph in the Foreword of the Royal Commission into Aged Care Quality and Safety Interim Report because it so clearly verbalises ageism that is unfolding in the Australian culture:

> It's not easy growing old. We avoid thinking and talking about it. As we age, we progressively shift our focus from work to the other things that give us purpose and joy: our children and grandchildren, our friends, our holidays, our homes and gardens, our local communities, our efforts as volunteers, our passions and our hobbies. The Australian community generally accepts that older people have earned the chance to enjoy their later years, after many decades of contribution and hard work. Yet the language of public discourse is not respectful towards older people. Rather, it is about burden, encumbrance, obligation and whether taxpayers can afford to pay for the dependence of older people. As a nation, Australia has drifted into an ageist mindset that undervalues older people and limits their possibilities.[21]

Ageism happens when someone treats you unfairly because of your age, and it plays a role in how we feel as we age. A friend reported an ageist comment overheard in the supermarket: 'Why don't these "oldies" shop during the week, when they have all the time they like, and leave the weekends to people who work to do their shopping?' This type of suggestion, that older people have nothing much to do and their time doesn't really matter, can be very demoralising.

The Australian Human Rights Commission highlights the systemic nature of age discrimination, with one of the many areas where ageism rears its ugly head being the workforce, and the impact this unlawful age discrimination has on the economic, social and psychological costs within employment.[22] Heather, a conversation participant, emphasises how the economic, social, and psychological impact of age discrimination influenced her life, particularly in her later years. Due to a period of ill health in her early 40s, Heather had to leave the workforce for a couple of years. When she was able to return to work, she had difficulty finding a job or the hours she needed to meet her financial commitments. Being underemployed with little income meant Heather had to sell her house and move to rental accommodation as she was unable to meet her mortgage repayments, and it meant she had less opportunity to build up her superannuation. Heather, now in her early seventies, is living on the age pension and has a *very* stringent budget to meet her basic costs of living. Life is restricting and psychologically stressful for her. Heather shared how she tries to manage living independently at home because she is not able to pay even the extra 'client contribution' required if she were to ask for home help or council gardening or cleaning support services.

Heather's situation is shared by Amy who, in her late sixties, is self employed as a health therapist and has therapy rooms in a large city centre. Due to the Covid-19 pandemic more people are working from home, leaving the large offices in the cities near empty. This has resulted in a huge drop in Amy's client numbers. She is struggling to meet rental payments on her city treatment facility as well as making the mortgage repayments on her home. Worry and anxiety loom large for Amy, unsure how, at her age, she can find the extra income needed to pay her bills. Heather and Amy express being perceived—more so as they are women—as 'too old' to be employed and they are each deeply concerned and stressed about their finances and moving into an ageing future. Both have voiced concern around having choices in and agency over future care or support services when the time comes. I wonder if we see, and will continue to see, more older workers facing redundancy because of the Covid-19 pandemic just like we saw following the global financial crisis. How can people over 65 be better supported with ongoing education and training within the work environment and how do we stop prejudice against older people in recruitment and retainment in the workplace?

Pascal's experience has been different, he acknowledged not being affected by ageism and finds himself 'very happy in the skin of an older person in my working life', but he goes on to say that he has found it 'interesting that many of the older, veteran members of my old department were the ones who've been moved out in recent years. That kind of ageism certainly seems to be rife in the marketing side of the agency, filled as it is with funky young folk.' After a period in retirement Pascal is now back in the workforce part time, and he mentions that it has been 'much easier for me to settle into the role of an interim regional tourism manager than some youngie. People look at this newcomer and by just looking at me and by doing the inevitable checking they come to a much readier willingness to listen to what I have to say. Having lots of life and career experience under one's belt is the privilege of the older person.' Pascal will not let ageism affect his life and work, but he does admit that he inadvertently participates in ageism and says:

> 'I have one guilty secret. I tend to treat young women aged anywhere up to their late 30s as my daughters! That's positive really—I look after them, make sure they feel well treated in the workplace as I'd like my daughters to be, etc. The downside of that is I find myself—gasp, choke—calling them 'love' on occasions as I do my daughters. Eep!'

I have not experienced much ageism directed towards me and if I do I will not let it affect me. However, I have witnessed a lot of condescending and patronising behaviour towards older people, particularly in health and aged care. My experiences are confirmed by a report on ageism conducted by the Benevolent Society in 2017, which identified health and aged care as key settings where ageism needs to be addressed. Some examples commonly witnessed within health and aged care include using belittling words such as 'dearie' or 'love' or the nauseating 'how are *we* today?', as well as by ignoring the older person or speaking to a family member instead of the older person while they are present, not respecting the person's wishes or needs in care, and taking away a person's rights and undermining their abilities.[23] This is, of course, not behaviour everyone experiences when engaging with health or aged care staff. Due to Merily's illness she regularly engaged with the health care system and her experience of interacting with health professionals have been positive: 'I am still strong minded and vocal enough to be heard when talking with health workers and have not had experiences of pressure, overtalking or disrespect'.

Ageism can go beyond these negatives, as gerontologist Salzman highlights in her article, 'Myths and Realities of Ageing': health concerns and symptoms in the elderly may at times be disregarded or considered part of the normal ageing process.[24] Consequently, several conditions in older adults are significantly under-diagnosed and under-treated due to ageism. Misconceptions about ageing frequently encountered in medicine and in society at large include issues involving sexuality, sleep disturbance, depression, cognitive impairment and substance abuse.

The Covid-19 pandemic has further exposed ageism. Older people and people living with disabilities have been more exposed to physical isolation and they were initially also dying at a disproportionate rate. While in many cases this was because they were physically more vulnerable, it was also because it seems they were seen as expendable. We saw and heard the stories of medical staff needing to make difficult decisions about who was eligible to receive intensive care in a scenario where there were more sick people than there was medical equipment to support all who needed lifesaving intervention.

EveryAGE Counts, a coalition set up specifically to challenge ageism against older Australians, reports an increase of ageist attitudes towards older people such as blame: due to 'the heightened susceptibility of older people to the virus and specific advice that they self-isolate is sometimes seeing older people blamed for the community-wide restrictions'.[25]

Merily drew my attention to a May 2020 podcast on ABC Radio National 'The Minefield' presented by Waleed Aly and Scott Stephens who discussed the ethical dilemma 'Is there a moral case against the Covid-19 shutdown'. This discussion came about because several philosophers had argued that there are deeply problematic and possible unethical aspects of the imposed lockdowns. With a focus on loss of life, particularly of the more vulnerable, and which and how many lives are to be sacrificed, the podcast considered whether there was a moral case against the shutdowns or whether there were other, more humane and democratic ways to protect the most vulnerable while also tending to the aspects of everyday life. The podcast clearly affected Merily, as she said:

> 'I heard a philosophical discussion on the ABC about the expendability of old people affected by the virus where a viewpoint was put forward, now that you are old and no longer useful to me and my emotional ties to you have thinned, what is the point of your life to me or society? This is how the herd mentality works as it is the old that are mainly affected. Very frightening to hear it vocalised as it has been considered. I think this is ageism at its worst.'

Pascal also commented on the experience of ageism around the coronavirus pandemic:

> 'The real main myth is that people in their seventies and eighties are inevitably 'old'. The coronavirus has underscored how so many of our children are the worst offenders! The amount of anxiety and censoriousness into admonishing their parents to be more careful! More than one friend is suffering grief because their children will not

let them see or hug their grandchildren—often out of concern for the oldies. I call it 'frailing'. We are not frail! We're robust! There were many debates around how to protect the more 'vulnerable' people within our population from the virus and discussions often happen without including the population in question, thereby making decisions *for* instead of making decisions *with* this cohort.'

The above-mentioned literary review by the Benevolent Society and the report by the Australian Human Rights Commission highlight the negative impacts of ageism on mental and physical health and the consequences for potential future participation opportunities within community and the workforce. We see an interesting dichotomy here: on the one hand we see older people who want to work and financially contribute, as in paying taxes, but age discrimination stands in their way, while on the other hand there are debates around the growing numbers of elderly and the claim that it is younger people who are going to pay for the increasing aged care costs … hmm, an interesting dilemma!

We see ageism in the language we use towards others and let us here consider journalism and written policies where ageing is seen as a problem or a burden, and in marketing where there is encouragement for the 'old to be young' when promoting a cosmetic product or procedure. Plus, we have the negative comments or thoughts from the public such as 'bumbling along', 'helpless', 'unproductive', 'cranky', 'senile', 'frail', 'disabled', 'unapproachable', 'childish' and 'demanding', to name but a few.

Three other aspects identified in the Benevolent Society report were attitudes and beliefs, behavioural discrimination, and formalised policy and practices. According to the studies, 'Ageism can be a self-fulfilling prophecy leading to internalised and reinforced perceptions of our own self-worth'.[26]

Does ageism begin with each of us? Ashton Applewhite believes so and says in her fabulous book *This Chair Rocks: A manifesto against ageism*:

'ageism begins between our own ears and is prejudice against your future self.' She encourages us to 'push back against ageism!'[27] I encourage you to watch her dynamic TED talk titled 'Let's end ageism'.[28] Internalised ageist attitudes show up in the manner in which we talk about ourselves and make comments such as: 'I am getting too old for this', 'I just don't understand technology and it is too late to learn', 'All old people have problems with memory', 'I am losing my balance because I am getting old'. We are not very kind towards ourselves; we tend to highlight the negative aspects of ageing such as declining and poor health, increasing dependency and financial concerns. So, what can we do to dispel these myths? Stand up and refuse to let an older person into your body and speak to you like that, is my advice!

We need to change the conversation about ageing and stop marginalising older adults. Let us instead highlight the unique gifts and contributions of older people as that will help to create a society in which older people are valued for their experience and integrated more into daily life. We are a great untapped resource.

Talking about gifts, I would like to return to the Covid-19 pandemic and ageing. Let me introduce you to Nipun Metha, founder of Servicespace, an incubator of gift economy projects that inspires people to be the change they wish to see. Nipun took part in telling stories of compassion in the time of the pandemic as part of the Presencing Institute Global Activation of Intention and Action (GAIA).[29] Nipun shared the story of 99-year-old UK veteran Tom Moore for his wonderful work raising funds for the National Health Service. Tom wanted to help and wondered how he could best do so. The veteran said that he could barely walk and used a walking frame, but he wanted to make a difference. His goal was to raise £1000 by daily walking up and down his backyard before he turned 100. However, once his story became public, this veteran raised £32 million for front-line health workers, and for his 100th birthday he received over 100,000 birthday cards and was knighted by the Queen for his contribution. Hey, what is old? This veteran, with his positive outlook and actions, was not 'too old' to make a difference.

Any form of 'ism' can be considered oppressive and polarising. We seem to have a mentality around 'us and them'. I wonder what stops us from being realistic and acknowledging that we are all humans, we are all in this life together? All of us are different, all unique, and we know and experience that, as human beings, we are interconnected. How do we overcome the polarisation that is ageism? Let's begin by first considering ourselves: am I perpetuating ageism? How do I experience and engage in ageism? Pull out your journal, consider your thoughts and notice the 'for' or 'against' qualities of your thoughts, words and actions. By becoming more aware, by noticing our thoughts and actions and by making positive steps to eradicating 'ism's' from our way of being, we will decrease polarisation within our communities.

Let's give a thought to ageism and gender. It is older women who face and deal with the accumulated effects of ageism and sexism. It is women who experience the dual discrimination in access to suitable and flexible employment and pensions, as was highlighted in the stories of Heather and Amy. It is women who seem to be having the dual informal care responsibility of looking after grandchildren and ageing parents, sometimes at the same time. It is women who predominate among caregivers for the elderly. For each of these comments I don't need to search for a reference, there are a multitude of stories. Delia, whom I have mentioned in the chapter on home and belonging and whose story you will read in chapter five, highlights her experience of ageism and gender. Delia's story is not unusual, it will resonate with many of you.

And these stories will resonate. Last week I heard this personal story from a woman who lectures at TAFE. She uses a fair bit of her annual leave to take her elderly father to medical appointments and, with her sisters and elderly parents, work out what future care is needed. She had mentioned a brother and yes, he does live nearby but seems to shy away from providing support and from engaging in conversations around future care decisions. In the last in-person conversation series, one participant in her late sixties could not attend the full series as her father became seriously ill and died, and it was up to her to take care of all his end of life needs and plan the funeral. Then there was the story of a woman who as a 'single' person had to place her needs aside as it was assumed that, as an unmarried daughter, she should take on the responsibility of caring for her mother who lived with dementia for many years. Her siblings had their own families and therefore were not as available! She shared with us her feelings of guilt and pain when the time came to place her mother into residential care. In that same group there was a woman who needed to leave each session early as she had grandparenting responsibilities to collect her grandchildren from school each day. And let's not forget the older women, a woman like Anne, who would rather suffer or go without, who may be unwilling to ask for help or who won't dare to complain as they 'don't want to be a burden' to their families. These are some of the stories I have heard, and there are many more, and to which I could add my own stories and experience of ageism and gender inequalities. It saddens and infuriates me to think about it. National Seniors published a report in 2020, 'Who Cares? Older Australians do', that highlights the informal and unpaid care needs provided by older Australians; gender inequality is also briefly discussed.[30]

For a recent (2021) look at what Australians think of older people, watch the SBS documentary 'What does Australia really think about old people?' It is emotional and confronting in places, and well worth watching.[31]

When research participants in the study conducted by the Benevolent Society were asked what a less ageist Australia would look like they reported the following:

Australians would have:
- greater empathy and compassion
- more knowledge transferred through the generations
- more tolerance, respect and acceptance

- happier, stronger and more connected communities.

In addition, older people would be more visible, active, productive and confident.[32]

Isn't that something we'd all like to see? While we need to accept the realities of ageing, we should not focus on getting older as the end phase. Rather, it is a new phase with new chances. Look forward to your ageing future, think ahead, look at all the possibilities and make plans. Consider your possibilities alone or with others. What can you still do on your own, what can you do and achieve with others? Change your mindset and embrace ageing with a zest for life as ageing does bring many beautiful moments and delightful opportunities. Explore some of the positive aspects of who you are and debunk the myths around ageism. Journal some of your thoughts. As I stated at the beginning of this book: Ageing is not a problem or a disease, ageing is living!

I will close this chapter with the following reflections from Fredrick Hudson:

I refuse to become a marginalised person! So many people just disappear, lose their nerve, and disconnect. Not me. I'm at the end of who I was. But I'm at the beginning of who I might become. That's exciting to me.[33]

CHAPTER 4

Money Matters

Money matters. *Too right*, money matters, but do we talk about money regarding ageing? So far in this book we have had conversations about home and belonging, the realities of ageing and ageism, and we have discussed how each of these topics influences our health and wellbeing as we age. Money matters too in each of these scenarios. For those of us who have less financial support, the need to plan is even more important. We talk about our wish to age in place, but it appears that older Australians are failing to plan for how they can remain living in their own homes. As Trev, a conversation participant said: 'I am not leaving my house as here is where I have lived most of my life, I belong here, and they will have to carry me out of that place in a coffin.'

Trev is not alone in his wish to die in his own home, as various reports including those from the Grattan Institute[34] and The Australian Centre for Social Innovation[35] consistently show that around 70 per cent of Australians would prefer to die at home rather than in a hospital or residential aged care—but the reality is that few older Australians die at home. According to a 2021 Australian Institute of Health and Welfare report, 'hospital (and this includes emergency departments) is the most common place of death for people 65 and over at around 50 per cent, residential aged care was the second most common setting accounting for 36 per cent and few older Australians (14%) died somewhere other than hospital or residential aged care settings.'[36] These data samples are from Victoria and Queensland. With Trev's wish to die in his own home it was good to have him and his wife join the conversation series with the intention of gaining some understanding about what they need to do to age well till the end of their days in their own home.

Living and dying in our own home may be our choice, but it does not always end up being the ideal option. Many—probably most—of us live in places that do not accommodate our basic needs. In chapter two we discussed whether your home is suitable for you to safely and independently age in place and considered retrofitting and other modifications. If that is the case for your future, do you have the financial means to modify your home? Let's consider the 'what ifs'. What if your mobility declined, for example, what would that mean, and would there be extra cost associated with this health change? I'll share with you the story of the shower in my bathroom. If I were to have a fall now and break a leg, I would not be able to have a shower because it is placed over the bath. Which means I must renovate my bathroom now, and that will cost money. Can I afford this expense? Or a story a friend shared: you are living in a well-designed level-floor house, most suited to 'age in place'. However, this very comfortable house is built on a hill, which means you have a steep or long inclined driveway and walkway to your house from street level. Not a problem if you can drive a car up this hill or deem walking up as a healthy and vigorous exercise, but what if you no longer drive and your ability to walk up this hill diminishes? Will you still be independently able to undertake all your activities of daily living such as shopping and attending social activities? If you wish to remain living in your home, would you have funds to install an inclinator or elevator from the street to your house if the need arises? Consider your options for living in small rural townships or even in suburbia, how our cars are important for us to get to our various activities of daily living such as work, shopping, leisure, sport and exercise, and social interactions. Can we afford to run and maintain a car, or indeed pay for taxis if or when we are no longer able to drive? If we have been cyclists, how long will we have the balance, strength, and confidence to keep pedalling?

The question arises: are we financially prepared to age and eventually die in our own homes? By this I mean we need to consider the broader perspective: is your living environment, your house, your garden, your community environment and community support services designed, suitable and affordable for you to live safely and independently at home till the end of your days? Are changes required and, if so, do you have the finances to make improvements, receive support or make contributions towards this? In addition to our own finances, is our government financially assisting us to age in place? Brodsky, Grey and Sinclair, in their article 'For Australians to have a choice of growing old at home, here is what needs to change', highlight the fact that many aspects of government policy in Australia in fact undermine successful ageing in place. They argue that, 'If governments want to promote active ageing, then older people must be given more flexibility in managing their assets. This means allowing them to sell the family home, take the tax-free asset value, downsize to a suitable smaller property, and put the leftover money into their super without penalties in the form of stamp duty, tax or loss of benefits.'[37] National Seniors Australia, an organisation which advocates on behalf of all older Australians, has an ongoing campaign which 'will fight for a retirement income system based on principles of adequacy, sustainability, certainty and fairness'.[38] See their website for more information, www.nationalseniors.com.au

The question raised above about how financially prepared we are to age and die in our own home is not one that Heather and Amy find easy to confront, due to the systemic ageism they experienced in retaining or obtaining work. Both are unable—or have limited ability—to financially plan or optimistically prepare for their ageing future. Are *you* financially prepared, are you able to afford the costs of home modifications, transport and possible outside help or care support services? Sadly, not many of us are according to a McCrindle Insights Report, which states that 'very few Australians aged 50+ are financially prepared for their future aged care'.[39] Nonetheless, if we wish to age and die in our home and community, we will need to make financial plans for our future.

According to the Australian Housing and Urban Research Institute (AHURI), 'supporting people to age in place is cost effective for our governments as the cost of service per person is significant lower when people stay in their own home', and they give the following example:

> a person assessing the Commonwealth Home Support Program (CHSP) cost the Commonwealth Government on average about $3,900 per person per year while the cost of a person living permanently in a residential aged care facility costs the Government around $69,055 each year (plus any costs paid by the aged care resident from their own pocket).[40]

I recommend you read the full article. Further, a Palliative Care Australia economic research note highlights evidence that:

> home-based palliative care saves financial resources while improving consumer quality of life and that person-centred palliative home care is cost effective ... It has been estimated that to double the number of older Australians dying at home would require an additional investment in palliative care of around $237 million a year [for 2013–2014]. When people die at home, major savings usually accrue from their reduced use of the hospitals and residential aged care ... [so] that funds released from the reduced need for institutional care offset the costs of providing palliative care to more people at home, making this a cost neutral policy.[41]

How do we advocate for extra support and funding to enable older Australians to fulfill their wish to live and die in their own home? As Australians, we may need to become more politically active!

Baby boomers, those of us born between 1946 and 1964, are the first generation to experience and enjoy what Sara Lawrence-Lightfoot calls the 'third age', the period in life of active retirement where people are 'neither old nor young'.[42] It is the 'new' development stage of life—for many a good twenty years—between a relatively healthy life after retirement and the beginning of age-related physical, emotional and cognitive limitations. These extra years in retirement change how individuals should consider and prepare for their economic and social wellbeing, as should our governments and employers.[43] Any economic decisions made now will also have their ripple effects onto future generations. Many of us in our youthful years took part in the struggle for rights for a myriad different groups. Perhaps we could now use that experience to fight against ageism and for a more equitable system to support ageing, a system that would not only help us live more comfortably, but also place less financial burden on future generations.

Money does matter and the reality is that it matters differently for each person reaching retirement age. The concept of retirement has long been portrayed as people stopping work at the age of 65, receiving a gold watch from their employer and a pension from the government, and taking to the golf course. But as we know this is rarely true. Here too, the scenario for everyone is different and not every person at the age of retirement has the same income or resources, or the same view on how to spend their years in retirement. Furthermore, we know that our financial status at retirement will have an impact on our health and social wellbeing. Recent changes in the law are moving the pension age to 67; this will take place over several years. Check the Department of Social Services website for details of how you may be affected, and of your eligibility for an Australian aged pension.[44]

Today, people are working longer and well past their 'retirement' age.[45] People may gradually shift from full-time work to part-time work before full retirement; others may never consider themselves retired. For some this is a choice as they enjoy and value the work they do. It provides them with a purpose and a meaningful, active role within society, and they likely enjoy the extra income. For others, working longer is a necessity as their superannuation savings or the pension is not sufficient to live on in retirement or they are carers, for their own ageing relatives, children or grandchildren. And then there are older people who are asset rich, as in owning the house they live in, but cash poor. For all these older Australians, the ongoing income that work provides is essential to support themselves and sometimes others.

This is particularly the case for women, who do not do as well financially compared to men, and many women cannot afford to retire or to retire early.[46] The levels of poverty and homelessness experienced by older women is high. Women often retire with half the amount of superannuation of men, as many took time out of work to raise children and/or received lower wages during their working lives due to salary inequality. And they are often the ones who take care of ageing parents or grandchildren. For men, it is more likely poor health that forces them out of paid work.[47] However, finding work as an older person—male or female—is difficult and age discrimination undoubtedly plays a huge role, as discussed in the previous chapter.

There is certainly a huge divide between the haves and the have-nots. While there are older Australians who can afford and will spend their money on products and services, by and large, according to Butler in his book on the politics of ageing, 'the financial security of older Australians is actually quite precarious'.[48] Pascal finds himself in this category. At age 72 he is back in the workforce on a part-time basis as is his wife Petra, who works 12 hours a week as an administration officer. They live a simple life, and both proclaim being frugal in their spending. 'No holidays, other than [pre-Covid] trips to Melbourne and Sydney to see our daughters.' They have a mortgage they are trying to pay off as fast as possible. Their son, still living with them, supports financially by paying board and this contributes towards bills such as power, water and rates. Any savings they may have go towards maintenance, repairs and upgrades to their house. Pascal reveals that he and Petra were never able to save money.

> 'We lived on one income for most of our married life and we had considerable health bills for two of our children, and we supported children through their poor student days. We also had to 'rescue' one of our daughters as she made disastrous decisions around a rental property to be used as a dance studio. This unfortunate scenario cost us around $90,000, which came from our mortgage. Also, we made unwise decisions to go with various superannuation schemes which we then had to cash in again when we needed cash urgently during the worst of our children's health emergencies. I lost my job in 2008 at the height of the financial crisis and our super plummeted again. Total super when I leave this job will be around $5k and for Petra when she retires it might have got up to say $15k. So, you could say, we haven't been or been able to be brilliant financial planners! And we still aren't.'

Pascal raises an interesting topic: 'the Bank of Mum and Dad'. Yes, I am aware that many parents support their children financially, as we do, but I had not realised that the Bank of Mum and Dad is 'the fifth biggest home lender in Australia'[49] to support their children with the purchase of (usually) their first home! This report also mentioned that, for many parents, it is causing financial strain and may cause them to have to work longer than they had imagined before retiring, as Pascal highlights.

In an ABC report (November 2019) the then Federal Treasurer Josh Frydenberg said that 'over the next four decades the number of Australians working and paying income tax for every person over the age of 65 will fall from 4.5 to 2.7', arguing that the proportion of people in the workforce would therefore have to grow substantially to make up the shortfall. 'The government needs people to keep working and paying income tax to offset spending on age pensions, health care and the like.'[50] These comments were made a couple of months before the coronavirus pandemic made an entrance into our world, which makes me wonder how many Australians can work now and pay income tax to offset the aforementioned costs?

That the Covid-19 pandemic most certainly had an impact on the finances of older Australians was reported by Bina Brown in an article in the *Financial Review*: 'Covid-19 puts squeeze on older Australians' finances.'[51] Older Australians are feeling the impact of Covid-19 on their finances, particularly if a decision has to be made about the feasibility of living at home with extra support, or whether residential aged care needs to be considered. There is ongoing concern among older Australians about the decreasing value of personal assets such as the home and personal savings, while on the other hand the cost for extra home support or residential care is increasing. However, since the publication of Brown's report in 2020 we see that house prices across Australia are actually soaring (as at late 2021), which means that it may be a good time to sell the family home if you are considering downsizing. Nevertheless, for people paying rent or wishing to buy another house, this increasing cost is a major concern.

I wonder, did you need to pay extra for help or services during the pandemic lockdowns, perhaps for help normally provided by family, friends or neighbours such as delivery of groceries and meals? Were you able to meet this increasing cost with the share market and super funds taking a massive hit and reducing your income options? And could you do so again if another global pandemic or crisis occurs? On top of the financial concerns in this time of pandemic there is also, for those who do need to move to residential care, the emotional and psychological stress of the move, particularly if potential helpers such as family and friends are in lockdown or unable to travel. Moving to residential care is, for most older people, a challenging and at times traumatic experience that requires a huge personal adjustment. During this pandemic the challenges were heightened by restrictions around personal freedom of movement and increased social isolation caused by restrictions on visitors.

Further, with the March 2021 release of the final Royal Commission into Aged Care Quality and Safety report, it is clear that a HUGE increase in funding is needed to build up and support the aged care sector.[52] In May 2021, the Treasurer delivered the Federal budget and promised $17.7 billion to bring about change in aged care in Australia. For a brief overview of what that entails look at the Australian Government Department of Health website.[53] This website provides links to more detailed information sites.

In its response to the problems outlined in the Royal Commission report, the Australian Government outlines five pillars of reform to be carried out over five years, and what are included in the key budget initiatives for that period.

The five pillars are:
1. at-home care and support: supporting Australians who wish to stay at home
2. residential aged care services and sustainability: improving and simplifying residential aged care services and access
3. residential care quality and safety: improving residential aged care quality and safety
4. workforce: supporting and growing a better-skilled workforce
5. governance: new legislation and stronger workforce.[54]

The big question is: will $17.7 billion be ultimately enough? Some local comments I have heard from people within the aged care industry say that $17.7 billion is only a drop in the ocean. The concerns expressed in these local comments were confirmed in an article in *The Guardian* in April 2021, 'Aged Care leaders worry Morrison government's budget boost will not be enough', that goes on to say, 'it's about a quarter of what's needed to address the findings of the Aged Care Royal Commission'.[55]

How, then, will we pay for it? According to a report by Coorey and McIlroy in the *Financial Review*, the Federal Government seems to be open to a tax increase to fund the reforms in the aged care sector and may consider the option of an income tax rise or an increase to the

Medicare Levy.[56] Currently, it is not clear if or how much an older person will be responsible for or required to co-contribute when needing aged care after the reforms are implemented.

Can we as older people afford the co-contributions when receiving aged care, and can we as a nation afford the likely increases in taxes and contributions towards Medicare and aged care support services? Contrarily, those wanting to work to help fund their later years are squeezed out of the job market by those who will have the financial responsibility of supporting them. How well will this be received by the Australian public? There have been—and are—ageist and begrudging remarks made around the 'burden' of having to financially support an aged care system for all the now-increasing numbers of ageing baby boomers and the strain this increase in costs will place on our economy. This has been highlighted by Emma Dawson, Executive Director of Per Capita, speaking to the COTA Australia National Policy Forum about the economic impact of ageism:

> when a group of people is repeatedly dismissed as declining in productivity by virtue of the fact that they are getting older, we end up with a pervasive narrative that older people are an economic burden on the rest of us.[57]

We do live in interesting and uncertain times. Each of us needs to consider our own situation, but we can also turn some attention to the wider situation and consider what we can do to help resolve these seemingly intractable dilemmas.

Money matters at every age and particularly as we move into older age and no longer earn an income to support ourselves. What needs to change? The Centre for Ageing Better, discussing work and finances, suggests the following:

> What needs to change? We need to be supported to have longer and more fulfilling working lives, gleaning the benefits of being in a good

job, which are not just limited to income and pension savings. For this sea-change to happen, employers must adopt age-friendly practices, such as stopping age bias in recruitment, improving provision of flexible working, supporting carers and those with health conditions, and continuing to offer training and progression for workers of all ages. For those who fall out of work and struggle to get back into the labour market, government and others need to provide support tailored to individual needs and circumstances.[58]

And although the Centre for Ageing Better is based in the United Kingdom, its recommendations apply equally here in Australia and were echoed by The Australian Centre for Social Innovation: 'Making work better and more available to older workers will benefit individuals, the economy and the state, now and into the future.'[59]

Merilyn is ahead on financial planning for her ageing future; she was and still is a solid financial planner.

> 'I was previously a finance manager and small business owner. The financial accounts of our family have always been left to me to manage, which is what I wanted. My partner and I have never argued about money, but always discuss large expenditure and investments.
>
> My mother was an uneducated migrant cleaner who worked early mornings with the sole aim of owning her own home to give her independence. This mantra was absorbed by me and I passed it on to my daughter, who purchased a unit when 19 years old.
>
> Property development was how my partner, who is a builder, and I built up some wealth but with the end focus to be debt free and self-supporting, which we achieved. However, we now fall into the category of asset rich and cash strapped. We receive a decent income from our rental properties but have found with increasing costs, what we had thought would be very comfortable including allowing overseas travel, is now just comfortable with a cap on our spending

for travel. Fixed costs (living expenses) take a surprising amount of the sum and saving is nearly non-existent though I have found, with self-isolation due to the virus, it has highlighted where money is wasted.

We have discussed selling assets and living on capital to free some cash. In this low interest climate, economically that is a poor option. After years of building up wealth there is a reluctance in both of us to eat into that capital, which is silly as its purpose is to support us in our older years. Old habits die hard.

It is not necessary yet to downsize and I would find that very difficult due to the emotional attachment. We intend to stay in our own home for as long as is possible and pay for support we need if possible. Planning about ageing means accepting your own mortality and the realism of a limited amount of time left, *but how much?* Preparing yourself for what could be very unexpected changes takes some courage and a willingness to be flexible if needed. I have some confidence that my daughter, who is a nurse, will do her best to help us manage important changes. That is a great comfort. We are comforted to know that, when necessary, due to health or frailty issues, we have funds that can be realised to cover relocation or aged care support.'

Merily's question of 'how much' is two-fold: how much time do I have left to live and how much do I need money-wise to live well to the end of my days? We do not know the answer to Merily's first question, although we are aware that we are living in the latter part, the third or fourth chapter of our lives. Therefore we need to consider and—to the best of our ability—work out what our future financial needs may be. As Merily says, preparing for your 'unknown' future does take courage and flexibility, but it is a task worth doing. Are you financially prepared for your ageing future? If financial planning is not one of your strengths, pay a financial advisor or accountant to help you work out your future financial needs—it is money well invested. Consider questions like what you may need money for, and what amount is needed to meet your current and ongoing costs.

Activity

I invite you to get pen and paper or, even better, get a large sheet of drawing paper and some coloured pencils or sticky notes. Draw on the sheet of paper a large tree and fill the branches with leaves (a money tree). On each of these leaves write something you will need to consider regarding your future ageing costs. Make a clear and honest accounting of expenses that you anticipate over the coming years and do these calculations in the context of some different living scenarios. What are alternatives, ideas or solutions? What and where are the costs? Where could you make some savings? Also consider the following questions:

- Have you done some financial planning?
- Do you have a budget?
- Are you or will you be living on a fixed income?
- How do you finance your lifestyle?
- What is your cost of living in your present situation?
- What are your housing costs?
- Is downsizing or right-sizing an option to consider?
- If so, how will that change your cost of living and lifestyle?
- What would your costs be in other ageing or housing scenarios? Include the cost of assisted care, retirement living, nursing home/residential care. Check out Bina Brown's article in the *Financial Review*.
- What do you perceive your future expenses to be?
- Have you discussed your finances or future care and living plans with your family and loved ones?
- If you are a couple: How will your loved one survive financially without you?

I wonder what your tree looks like at the end of this activity. Were there any surprises for you?

Plan your financial future so you can live independently for as long as possible. Consider your own financial, physical, and emotional wellbeing and work out what funds you would need to age well and with enjoyment at home into the future. As I mentioned earlier, it is well worth considering paying for a professional financial adviser, particularly one who has expertise in aged care planning.[60]

Money and other financial assets, good health and wellbeing, and personal independence are important for how you move into and experience ageing well into the future. A lack of money means less choices: but no matter how small your savings and assets, you need to make the most of them so that you can have as much control as possible over your future.

I hope that this chapter on Money Matters will spark conversations within your friendship circle and family and among your peers as they are important conversations to have. We need to accept that we are getting older and that one day we will be OLD, as in likely to be needing support for health and aged care. I encourage you to do your homework, find out the facts around costs and eligibility for government financial support if and when required, act and get your finances in order. Most future support or care you will need costs money as we will see in our next chapter on care and care support.

CHAPTER 5

Care and Care Support

True help is an art.
—Hilary Cottam, *Radical Help*

In the last chapter we explored what you need to consider financially as you move into your ageing future. I wonder if you took potential future care costs into consideration; if so, what do you expect your future care costs to be and who will pay for and provide these services? Data shows that two-thirds of older Australians expect their future care costs to be $400 per week or less, and nearly half intend to subsidise the expenses with government payments. More than one in six expect the government to fully fund their future care.[61] According to the McCrindle report, it is expected that in 2048 (less than 30 years from today) there will be 7.5 million Australians aged over 65, with average life expectancy approaching 90. In the meantime, the worker ratio is declining, which puts extra pressure on the economy and demands on the workforce.[62] It is a fact: our population is ageing and there are numerous baby boomers already over the age of 65. The question arises: if older Australians are putting off planning due to unrealistic expectations of aged care costs and expectations that government will largely pay the bill, can our economy afford those care bills and what would that mean for *you* in the future? On a more positive note, a recent report by Ratcliffe, Chen, Khadka et al. for the Royal Commission into Aged Care Quality and Safety revealed that 'the majority of current income taxpayers (61%) indicated that they would be willing to pay more income tax to support aged care',[63] which is promising.

Let us not forget the many contributions that older Australians make, in volunteering a lot of their time in service to others in their community. I have met several conversation participants, aged in their mid sixties, who provide care and other support to their frail ageing parents and who also have a grandparenting responsibility for their grandchildren. Numerous others have volunteer roles within community organisations, each playing an important role and making a huge contribution to the economy. This generation needs to be recognised as an asset and not as a burden to our economy.

It is a certainly the case that as we get older our bodies and minds deteriorate, that things we used to do with ease are not so easy anymore. When was the last time you were sick? Who helped you out? What would it mean if you become one of the 25 per cent of ageing Australians who will need some level of assistance in your daily life?

In the book *Connect: Design for an empathic society*,[64] I came across reference to an animated story: *Charlie and Marie: A tale of ageing*.[65] I encourage you to watch it as it tells a story about very realistic ageing events which can occur from the age of 60 and the challenges associated with these significant health and wellbeing events. The narrative is about Charlie and Marie's interactions with the numerous health, aged care and support services and although this animated story comes from Europe, we will all recognise similarities experienced here in Australia.

McCrindle's 2018 study shows that 75 per cent of older Australians have not taken any steps to ensure they will receive their preferred future care. Thirty per cent of older Australians have been involved in organising care for a parent but they are having to make decisions quickly with limited information. The process of organising care for a parent is most often triggered by a sudden event causing ill-health or injury (41%)

with 40 per cent spending less than one month actively exploring care options.[66]

Delia found herself in this situation when the health and wellbeing of both her parents suddenly declined. Delia shares her personal observations of a period of 18 months with the hope that her experience will prompt others to have conversations with parents about ageing well and about being informed and making plans for future care.

> 'My life changed dramatically due to family needs 18 months ago [in December 2017] and historically there was no discussion or plan in place to enable me to envisage what my future was about to hold.
>
> There is no theoretical substitute for personally being immersed in the experience, but areas I needed to research, explore, and attempt to process under pressure are included in the following:
>
> My parents Daisy and Archie were an active, independent and community minded couple, aged 87 and 92, who had lived for 66 years in the same small home with a large, loved garden. They were described as a dynamic couple who had been aging well for 20 years and more. My mother often reflected on a disappointing crossroad 35 years ago when the decision had been made for her to focus on her art career, then her father died, and she felt her siblings had willed her into the role of carer for their mother.
>
> Their Plan A was to stay in their own home until they died ... they had a will and my brother and I had enduring power of attorney, but no advance care directive or instructions for funerals.
>
> They believed that my father, being 5 years older, would die first, so my mother continued to place his needs first, as is typical of the generation. He had retired at 59 whereas my mother was still carrying the same domestic load at 87 as she did at 27 years of age. Talk of home support was rejected as intrusive and disruptive to the status quo ... this was voiced mainly by my father.

Suddenly there was a situation for which there was no plan and we had no experience as a family. My mother was diagnosed with terminal cancer. In the following 8 months until her death, my brother had a heart attack, my sister-in law lung cancer and my father renal surgery and 5 weeks hospitalisation.

Out of the five of us, four would spend time in hospital and 3 in a high dependency ward. Out of the five of us, two were happily working in their long-term professions. Out of the two of us working, one was a male medical specialist and one a female medical technologist.

What happened next? Nothing unpredictable as this scenario is shared by many. Families develop modes of normal functioning, overlooking differences and allowing space between members where required. 'The wheels falling off', when an elderly member has a significant medical event, creates a compressive environment, the family is forced together at an anxious, emotional time and the differences between people magnify.

So, if you wish to live as independently in your own home for as long as possible, who in your family may be selected to step in during a medical crisis? Can your family engage in open discussions about uncomfortable situations before a crisis occurs? Will family members support each other or [be in] conflict?

Situations can unravel very quickly, and I found myself sleeping in my childhood bed still in work clothes early in the nine months. The topics of who had the more important job and expectations on older females to take the load for the family were voiced ... It was fortunate for the family as I was able to leave work one lunchtime, incrementally use 14 weeks long service leave and eventually resign/retire.

During an early hospital stay we were able to commence My Aged Care assessments for my parents and, as it transpired, my mother had been wanting them both to do this for some time. On her return home an individual family member helped her complete her advance care directive. I read it at the time of witnessing and noted that her wishes were to be cared for in the family home and to die in her own bed supported by her family.

The family home was fitted with safety rails, personal medical alert alarms, toilet raisers and shower chairs. Meals were ordered for the week. Medical tests and treatment had adverse effects resulting in hospitalisations for both parents at different times. My father no longer felt as confident that he could support my mother in her decreasing stability but simultaneously resented the intrusions into their home and the changes to life as they planned it. They felt a loss of privacy, dignity, and mobility they had hoped to avoid by staying in their own home.

My father was rushed to hospital, not returning for five weeks, so the financial management of the house needed to be organised, the dog needed care. By now most of the activities of daily living for my mother had to be done for her and there were falls and collisions in the small hallways. The palliative nursing team visited twice weekly. The house was not suitable for in-home overnight care so we created a roster system where I had every 3rd or 4th night off and an elderly aunt would sleep in the same single bed.

The personal mental and physical load was immense on all involved. I was practiced in my workplace to work under pressure and accept responsibility for decisions, but this new role of carer was an 8-hour shift that never ended, without a way of measuring success. The new role of carer overshadowed the existing parent and child relationship.

After five weeks in hospital my frail 93-year-old father was to be discharged home with almost daily nursing visits. He felt confident that he could regain his strength alone but not with my mother's accelerating care requirements. The decision was made to use the newly acquired My Aged Care, High Level Respite Care code to access a room in a facility for two weeks.

Finding an available room is a challenge but we were fortunate to gain a place in our first choice, close to the family home and with the family GP visiting. Only my mother could not understand the need for her to go and felt betrayed, as this was not following her advance care directive wishes.

I was the person who was caring for her at home, packing and admitting her to the facility so she saw me as responsible for her situation, although this was extended to my father early over the following three months. He arrived home the day after she was admitted and commenced a new routine of daily visits to her in amongst his own schedule of infusions and medical checks.

Respite Care is structured for the short term, so extensions are not guaranteed [automatically] and need to be renegotiated every two to three weeks to a limit of 81 days. As [my mother] deteriorated there were many phone calls and anxious times waiting for return calls to ensure the family had the next two weeks covered and it was only ten days before her death that she gained permanency in the facility. My mother, an active church member, died without instructions for her funeral.'

8 months later

'My father lives independently in the house and garden he loves, with the support of family and neighbours. He welcomes the relationships he has developed with shopping and cleaning home support people. He has returned to the routines he shared with my mother and washes, irons, remembers birthdays, rings friends, and buys flowers for the house. He still has engaged conversations with the dog.

He sometimes wakes in the night and wonders if he was a good husband.

My father does not have an advance care directive nor instructions for his funeral and is known to climb ladders and not hear the phone.

He is living as he planned.'

Delia's story is far from unique and her struggles with the system and feelings of loss, guilt and frustration around care provision resonate with many other family members, sons, and daughters or friends of older Australians. Regarding future care, who will provide the person-centred care for their Mum, Dad or dear friend while continuing to see these people as individuals with needs and wishes?

Most older people are confident that they will be looked after by their children or others when the time comes. Like Delia's parents, they speak about a daughter or son who lives nearby and who pops in daily to provide the extra support they need. It is the family who will take their elderly parent to the shops, hairdresser and medical appointments, and it is the family who will do most of the extra tasks around the house. In some scenarios, they pre-cook all meals and leave these in fridge or freezer for their parent to heat up at mealtimes. However, it is interesting to note that our longevity has coincided with the increased dependence of young families on dual incomes, with a result that the provision of extra care for an ageing parent is more challenging and stressful for all involved. Also, we are much more mobile as a population in recent years, and many families will be dispersed across the globe.

Anne, my neighbour whom I introduced you to earlier, is only just managing to be self-reliant in her independent living unit at the retirement village. She receives no support services and relies for all her care and social support on her daughter. However, Anne's daughter still works full-time and is feeling stressed at having to provide for all her mother's needs. Anne, in turn, shared that she is feeling increasingly lonely and depressed, but she does not want to be a further burden by asking her daughter for more support.

So, who will look after you when you are old and frail? Who will care for you when you need it? Have you given it some thought, or do you find it hard to believe that you will need help and support when you are frail, unwell, and struggling with your normal day-to-day activities? Pascal admits he has no idea, has not thought about it much and believes that his and Petra's plan is not to plan too much! 'Although', says Pascal:

> 'In general terms I would want to be cared for in the context of my loved and loving family and the familiar home environment. We anticipate that our three daughters will want to give back to their parents after our decades of active and often arduous support for them. But for now, there are too many other interesting or challenging things to deal with. *Manyana!*'

In preparing her advance care directive, Merily considered the options of asking her children for support when illness and frailty started to impact on her life. 'But what unnecessary burdens and distress could be placed on them in the final stages of life?' Merily said. She has not registered with My Aged Care for an assessment of her eligibility for care, although she could see the benefit, nor has she taken the important step of registering for some council support with home maintenance. However Merily says, 'I don't believe much reliance can be made on getting government assistance. The press indicates that there are long waiting lists for home assistance and care support. I am glad I have family and friends.' Merily is considering the 'what if's' and is clearly working through her options, while also keeping family and friends in mind to call on when need be.

Who will you call on when managing without help is no longer possible? Will you rely on your children, if you have them, or other close family members? Are you handing the decisions about your future care over to them? Is this realistic, is it fair to them, and is it likely to provide you with the care and support *you* want for yourself? As Pascal said, if the need for care arises, he would like to be cared for at home by his family. 'But', he adds,

> 'I'm also very aware of friends wilting under the pressure of looking after self-avowedly independent elderly parents who are anything but elderly. And given that my children would be dealing with the pressures of parenthood themselves I'd be very alert to causing them undue stress. I've assumed Petra has gone before me—although as she's 8 years younger it's more likely to be the other way around. In such a situation I've imagined myself quietly and firmly demanding to be placed—after the usual higher level of home care support that's available—in a home of some kind, no matter how crappy. I've lived a privileged life, one much more comfortable and fortunate than the great mass of humankind and a lot better than huge numbers of Australians. So, a less than wonderful context for my last years would be just a bit of balancing of the ledger.'

The stories from Delia, Anne, Pascal, Merily and many others highlight the evidence that the current care model of adult children providing that level of assistance may seem to be a simple solution, but it is increasingly not sustainable financially or emotionally. We need to acknowledge and support family members and other unpaid providers for all they do to support and care for their loved one. Their physical and emotional health is often affected by their caring duties, as this group of carers falls into the high-risk category for social isolation and loneliness, which we will discuss in our next conversation. For some family carers, often daughters, there is an added loss of income while taking on the full-time care role for their parents, as was highlighted in Delia's story. We have fewer children today compared to our parent's generation, our spouse may not be able to support us (we could be their carer) and our children do not always live nearby. All of that is assuming we have a spouse and children, which is far from the case as there is also an increase in people living alone.

This conversation is about care and support, about care receiving *and* care giving as you are getting older and frailer. What supports healthy ageing? Who will support us and where do we go for help if living life is becoming more challenging and managing without help is no longer feasible?

Finding some more support with your day-to-day tasks, transport, respite care while family or your carer is away or if a move to an aged care facility needs to be considered is not an easy nor necessarily enjoyable task. It is wise, well before you need any support, to explore where information is available and how you would go about making enquiries to get the support you need if and when that time comes. Being knowledgeable about what is available will take a lot of pressure and angst out of this stressful process. Jean Kittson provides some suggestions in her book *We Need to Talk About Mum and Dad: A practical guide to parenting our ageing parents* (2020).[67] It is an informative guide to supporting yourself or your parents when ageing well requires more support. This book, however, takes it one step further and says 'Mum and Dad, we *all* need to talk about ageing'!

There is an expression: 'It takes a village to raise a child', and there is now an innovative movement around the world focussing on senior housing and local communities with the motto 'It takes a village to "Age in Place"'! The meaning of that statement prompts the question: have you ever helped someone else out when they were ill?

There are several social innovations with respect to care happening around the world, such as co-healing, co-caring, and village-to-village or senior community hub networks. Co-healing and co-caring are terms used in senior co-housing communities.[68] Combined, they promote positive, active ageing.

Co-healing is about staying emotionally healthy through being part of a community or living within a supportive neighbourhood. The basic principles for remaining healthy as you age are eating a healthy diet, and being physically active and socially well connected, preferably with people who live nearby. We talk more about the importance of social connection for health and wellbeing in the next chapter. This is the important part: connecting with the people who live nearby in your neighbourhood and community, the people you see on a very regular basis, in the street, at the library or the community centre. We need to use these opportunities to talk together about day-to-day issues, the social incidentals, a form of communication we may use with our group at the local gym, our book club, craft group or 'coffee gang'. It is these others in our neighbourhoods who play a role in keeping us healthy.

I wonder if you have heard of Blue Zones. A Blue Zone is a non-scientific term first used by Dan Buettner for geographic regions that are home to some of the world's oldest people.[69] Buettner highlights nine life lessons which form the lifestyle habits of these longest-lived people:

1. move naturally
2. have a purpose in life
3. downshift: have regular routines to offload stress
4. 80 per cent rule: stop eating when your stomach is 80 per cent full, or eat less
5. plant slant: eat a higher plant-based diet
6. wine: drink in moderation
7. belong: be part of a community
8. the power of love
9. stay socially connected.[70]

Blue zones are areas which *design* for solutions to achieve a healthy and caring community. Have a look at the Blue Zone website: www.bluezones.com for it provides information on some of the topics we also discuss in this book.

Co-caring is a grassroots model of neighbourly support, where you look out for your neighbour and support each other in ways you have discussed and agreed upon, such as:

- checking at a certain time each day to see if the curtains are open, and ringing or coming over if they are not
- giving a key to the neighbour to check if you are ok if the curtains are not open at the agreed time
- swapping phone numbers and contact details of family members, close friends and GP
- picking up prescriptions from the chemist or some groceries from the supermarket
- giving a lift to the library, medical appointments or the shops
- bringing over an occasional meal
- checking mail or watering plants when you are away.

Co-caring supporters are neighbours or friends living nearby who will care for you when needs be. Co-caring provides support, and it helps to reduce loneliness and social isolation. This support is given on a voluntary basis, consisting of activities you are willing to do and have agreed to undertake for each other. It is a two-way street and of benefit to both the giver and the receiver. Co-caring encourages independence through awareness that we are all interdependent. As Merily says:

> 'I would feel happy and privileged to be of assistance to older friends and community members where physically possible and it is one of the attractions of the community knowing someone is keeping an eye out and where we could reciprocate in our support to each other.'

A supportive co-caring model can ensure social connection within your community or neighbourhood, which helps older people to stay in their homes and communities longer and out of institutional care as they age. In the Netherlands there is an expression: 'it is better to have a good neighbour than a faraway friend'. I am sure we all know wonderful examples of good neighbourhood support and care.

A more formalised form of co-caring and co-healing is the 'village' model of supporting older people who wish to age in place. The first of these village models, Beacon Hill, was established in Boston, USA, in 2002 by a group of friends and neighbours as a mutual support arrangement. Village-to-Village Networks, an umbrella organisation, states that villages are 'leading the way for a more economically efficient model for aging'. It describes them as 'grassroots, community-based organizations' that promote neighbour to neighbour support. 'Local Villages connect members to a full range of support services to help with non-medical household tasks, services, programs, and transportation. Villages also promote staying active by coordinating recreational, social, educational, and cultural programs.'[71] The Village-to-Village Network was established in 2010 and there are now more than 250 open villages and more than 100 villages in development around the world.[72] Currently, there is one Australian member of Village-to-Village Network; called Connect Victoria Park, it is operating in Perth.[73]

The first Australian seniors' hub was established in 2013 in Sydney, New South Wales, the Waverton Hub. It is:

> a mutual organisation of residents of Waverton, Wollstonecraft, and neighbouring areas in Sydney. As we grow older, we members of the Hub are helping each other to enjoy our lives, stay in our own homes for as long as we can, to be as healthy as we can, and achieve all this for as little cost as possible. We are ageing meaningfully in our own community.'[74]

About a dozen people started the organisation in late 2012 and it opened for membership in 2013 with a program of activities; by the end of April 2015 it had more than 300 members. Around 80 members are working on continuing to build the Hub, setting up systems, and designing and leading activities and events. The Australian Government has made a grant available for the Waverton Hub to assist other Australians in setting up new hubs in their town or neighbourhood. For information about setting up a senior hub, see their website where you can download the Waverton Hub Manual.

It would be wonderful to see other senior hub networks like the Waverton Hub and Connect Victoria Park emerging throughout Australia—community supporting community, building a strong network together. The Australian Government's My Aged Care website has a lot of information about aged care support but does not provide helpful information about local services. Pascal has no real idea who to contact if he requires information and extra support.

'We know our way generally around systems—although every new part of the health and welfare systems is a bewildering maze. At any rate we've many friends who've already had to delve into the system for their parents or partners and we'd drawn on their expertise.'

Another concept to assist people ageing in place is a community Circle. I learned about this concept in Hilary Cottam's book *Radical Help*. Cottam's passion is bringing about social change for a more just and caring society. She works in collaboration with people and communities in South London to make changes to the welfare state and thereby help improve people's quality of life. Circle is an innovative community-driven project established in 2018 for older people. It is a low-cost model which provides social connections, kindness, care and practical support to older people.[75]

I have a personal vision to establish what I would call a Place to Connect; it would have a welcoming shop front located in the main street of a town, village or suburb. People would see a friendly café and community hub where they could walk in off the street, have a cuppa, meet people and find out local information on health, wellbeing, social activities, volunteering and ageing in place, specific aged-related activities, services, and support programs, and have access to the My Aged Care portal. The Place to Connect will be about connecting, informing, serving, sharing, learning, and helping.

In my vision, this Place to Connect will have:

- a welcoming host (maître d') who is knowledgeable about aged care and support services and a good communicator, a person who is a supportive and enthusiastic community connector
- a professional who can provide more specific and detailed advice on support, services and pathways to assistance
- volunteers, for peer-to-peer services or to staff specific areas in the Hub
- local allied health and legal professional consultation services to support ageing in place
- peer-to-peer service exchange networks, such as a senior hub or a circle
- tutorials and hands-on workshops on using different and emerging technologies to their full advantage.

We must work together to respect, include and support our elders as they are a valued and integral part of our community. So, why not, as a community, open a Place to Connect where older people and their families can find helpful information about *local* services. A Place to Connect would also provide opportunities for older community members who are interested and able to offer their services to others. Such an exchange of skills will tick so many boxes: the feeling of belonging, social connectedness, giving life meaning, being seen and valued, and developing a sense of a positive future! A good friend and gerontologist encouraged me to consider including all members of the community in a Place to Connect. 'Why not,' she said, 'provide information and support to young parents, new immigrants, or new residents to the area?' Why not indeed! It is a great idea and has lots of possibilities.

Our current aged care model

There are a few community models of aged care, but the most extensive and well-known models are the various packages of care funded by the Australian Government. These cater for Australians aged 65 years and over or 50 years and over for Indigenous Australians, who are no longer able to live safely without support. The aged care services are available to eligible people and provided in the person's home, in the community, or in residential aged care facilities managed by a wide variety of licensed aged care providers. In the current situation (pending reforms following the Royal Commission into Aged Care Quality and Safety), the Australian Government funds Regional Assessment Services (RAS) and Aged Care Assessment Teams (ACAT) to provide the initial assessment services that determine eligibility. To receive the initial assessment services and subsequent non-urgent support, people must register with My Aged Care https://www.myagedcare.gov.au. All providers of care services, including for-profit and not-for-profit organisations, need to be registered under the Aged Care Quality and Safety Commission Act 2020,[76] and, when registered, list their services in the 'Find a provider' tool, which helps people find a suitable provider within their local area.[77]

The services currently available are:

- *Entry-level assistance*, offered through a Commonwealth Home Support Program (CHSP), is subsidised by government but recipients pay a fee for services. It includes allied health and therapy services, nursing, personal care, respite care, social support, provision of meals, local social activities, transport assistance, domestic assistance, home modification and home maintenance, goods and equipment and assistive technology. Links to housing and care services for people experiencing homelessness are also available (though these are short-term only). Service providers deliver care and services to recipients at a subsidised price. After you are assessed, the waiting period for assistance will depend on the availability of service providers in your area and there could well be a lengthy waiting period.
- *Home Care Packages* (HCPs) are delivered by approved providers, following an assessment via My Aged Care. Recipients are allocated a home-care package and associated funding level (there are 4), and work with their chosen provider to identify their

care needs and decide how best to spend the funding package. However, we have already reached the stage where demand has outstripped supply and the current (November 2022) waiting time of 3-6 months for level 1, 2, 3 and 4 packages.
- o Level 1 supports people with basic care needs
- o Level 2 supports people with low-level care needs
- o Level 3 supports people with immediate-level care needs
- o Level 4 supports people with very high-level care needs.
- *Transitional Care Packages* (for out-of-hospital care only) provide services for between 6 and 12 weeks per year and are designed as a rehabilitation and re-enablement program. To qualify for these services a person is assessed in hospital by the Aged Care Assessment Team (ACAT), and they must have completed their acute or subacute care, be medically stable and ready to be discharged from hospital.
- *Respite care* is short-term residential care (for up to 6 weeks per year), usually to give a carer some respite. Eligibility is assessed during a face-to-face assessment organised through My Aged Care Regional Assessment Services (RAS)
- *Residential care* in residential aged care facilities is for older people who are no longer able to live independently at home and need ongoing help with everyday tasks or health care that is available 24 hours a day. Residents are able to stay until their end of life or can leave if they wish. Once a person is assessed as eligible, it is usually their carer or family who arranges entry directly with the aged care facility. Entry also depends on whether there is a bed available, which is why there can be very limited choice if a decision has to be made urgently.

I highly recommend you and your family do your homework and check out the My Aged Care web site: https://www.myagedcare.gov.au as it contains a wealth of information. It is best to be well informed about all the costs and choices before decisions need to be made. All Home

Care Package providers must publish their prices on the My Aged Care website.

Older Australians and their families have mixed views on the aged care received via these services at home and in residential care. Numerous reports by family members of abuse and neglect of their loved ones in residential care prompted the Australian Government in October 2018 to appointment a Royal Commission into Aged Care Quality and Safety. The interim report was released in October 2019 and final report in March 2021. The interim report of the Royal Commission into Aged Care does not make you feel good about becoming an older person and needing care. There are, however, positive stories about older people being treated with respect and dignity, hopeful stories where personal care and support goals and needs are met by staff who are well trained and caring. Sadly, there are also numerous heartbreaking and horrendous stories of disrespect, abuse and neglect.

> The Royal Commission has heard compelling evidence that the system designed to care for older Australians is woefully inadequate. Many people receiving aged care services have their basic human rights denied. Their dignity is not respected and their identity is ignored. It most certainly is not a full life. It is a shocking tale of neglect.[78]

In its final report the Royal Commissioners made 148 recommendations for the fundamental reform of the aged care system. You can read these on its website.[79]

A media release on 28 July 2022 by the Hon Anika Wells MP, Federal Minister for Aged Care, stated that the delivery of a reformed and improved in-home aged care program would be provided by 1 July 2024, the date contained in recommendations from the Royal Commission final report.[80]

This should be a wake-up call for all of us. To genuinely help people with living life on their own terms is harder to do than to talk about.

The questions that need to be asked include: What does the older person want? Am I, as care-giver, truly meeting *their* needs or am I meeting *my* needs or time schedule? One of my clients mentioned to me one day that she makes sure she is showered and dressed before her personal carer—whose job it is to assist her with these tasks—arrives. Why was that? I asked her. Her reply is very telling:

> 'The carer rushes me so much that when showering and dressing are done, I am completely breathless, utterly exhausted, and unable to enjoy other activities in my day. By getting up early and taking my time with showering and dressing I am feeling less depleted.'

What a sad story! In a situation like this it is easy to feel that you are the weaker party, that you don't want to or are fearful of upsetting the care giver—especially if you are not used to speaking up for yourself. It is situations like these when we need a friend or advocate to help us speak up and insist on better care. This practice needs to change dramatically to ensure a truly person-centred outcome. How do we turn these negative experiences into positive ones? What is our role, as the recipients of care, to ensure that, when the need arrives, we receive improved and respectful services by well-trained carers and professionals? Do we leave the decision making up to our children or others? If we wish to live our lives on our terms, we will need to take on some of the responsibility, which means: think about it, talk about it with others, and inform ourselves.

How to best support a person in need of care or support—the words of the Danish philosopher Soren Aabye Kierkegaard really speak to me in this regard. Here is what he said:

> If one is truly to succeed in leading a person to a specific place, one must first and foremost take care to find him where he is and begin there.

> This is the secret in the entire art of helping.

Anyone who cannot do this is himself under a delusion if he thinks he is able to help someone else. In order truly to help someone else, I must understand more than he—but certainly first and foremost understand what he understands. If I do not do that, then my greater understanding does not help him at all. If I nevertheless want to assert my greater understanding, then it is because I am vain or proud, then basically instead of benefiting him I really want to be admired by him.

But all true helping begins with a humbling.

The helper must first humble himself under the person he wants to help and thereby understand that to help is not to dominate but to serve, that to help is not to be the most dominating but the most patient, that to help is a willingness for the time being to put up with being in the wrong and not understanding what the other understands.[81]

In this chapter we talked about care and care support—the provisions of care as well as the receiving of care. You, like me, may have had the opportunity to support or care for an older family member, friend, neighbour or taken on this role as a volunteer within the community. The time will likely come, sooner or much later, when we ourselves need some extra support or care. Coping with change is difficult and there will be an experience of loss. Getting older is not always an easy journey but how we deal with and grow from these changes is often a key factor to healthy ageing. Therefore, consider options and be pro-active about future care as that enables you to have the best life possible, right to the very end!

CHAPTER 6

The Importance of Social Connections

As people, young or old, most of us are by nature social creatures who thrive by connecting with each other. Human connection needs to have that 'just right' balance between the freedom to be independent and the feeling of being emotionally linked to other human beings. In our last conversation about care and support, the importance of a 'village' to age in place was highlighted. Living in a supportive, interdependent neighbourhood and community, where people of all ages look out for and support one another, helps to make ageing alone for longer possible. Relating to people around us plays an especially important part in our feelings of wellbeing.

There are many studies that show that there is a direct correlation between good social connections and wellbeing. A decrease in social connections tends to show a decline in wellbeing and increase in loneliness, which in turn can lead to depression. However, it is important to note that people who are socially isolated do not necessarily feel lonely and, conversely, we can feel very alone and lonely while surrounded by people. Most of us enjoy connecting and engaging with others. Our minds need healthy social connections just as our physical bodies needs nutritious food.

Parker Palmer in his book 'A Hidden Wholeness' speaks about how solitude and community go together: 'we need both the interior intimacy that comes with solitude and the otherness that comes with community'.

'We have too much to learn from within, but it is easy to get lost in the labyrinth of life. We have much to learn from others, but it is easy to get lost in the confusion of the crowd. So we need solitude and community simultaneously: what we learn in one mode can check and balance what we learn in the other. Together, they make us whole, like breathing in and breathing out'. -

'Solitude does not necessarily mean living apart from others; rather it means never living apart from one's self'. -

'Community doesn't necessarily mean living face-to-face with others; rather it means never losing the awareness that we are connected to each other'.[82]

According to the Australian Institute of Health and Welfare, social isolation and loneliness are experienced by *all* age groups and are a growing public health issue facing communities in Australia.[83] The Centre for Ageing Better makes mention that, with a rising number of people in their fifties and sixties alone or divorcing, community structures are changing. This in turn has implications for the role of communities in ensuring that people remain connected and supported.[84] Another highly vulnerable group at risk of social isolation and loneliness are the people (often in their fifties and sixties) who provide extended hours of informal care to their loved ones, friends or neighbours at home. This is due to their decreased social interaction with others while in the carer role, as we touched on in our last conversation on care and support.

This also raises another concern: what would happen if, as an informal carer in your fifties, sixties or older, you are no longer able to provide that care? This could be due to illness or injury or because you are physically and emotionally exhausted from providing regular care. In that situation, who would take on the caring role for the person you provide care to? What future caring arrangements do you need to consider when you are no longer able to carry on or you wish to retire from this caring role? What plans can you and do you need to put in place for when that time comes?

Back to our conversation on the importance of social connections. In the older and more vulnerable population, 75 to 80 plus years, social isolation and loneliness are on the increase and, according to research, their detrimental health impacts can be as bad as smoking 15 cigarettes a day![85] As we age, we face many life changes, some drastic. Not only do our bodies begin to deteriorate, but our social interactions become more difficult as well. Due to our physical decline, we may not be able to walk any distance, or we may no longer have a driver's licence. We may find it more tiring or painful to engage with others and have to limit our social activities. A partner, family or friends we once had to lean on may have died or may be themselves in a situation where they can no longer support us and are themselves needing extra support. Our children or other loved ones are often busy with their spouses, children, careers or health issues and therefore are not always available to engage on a social level or provide the support we would like. Social isolation can quickly become a reality for each of us and for a variety of reasons. Whatever the cause, the feelings of being left alone and vulnerable are painful and, if not changed, can lead to depression.

All levels of government see social isolation and loneliness as significant health and wellbeing issues and are looking at wide-ranging initiatives to socially engage the older population with an aim to reduce loneliness and its corollary, depression. Social interaction for older adults is important for numerous reasons, from physical to emotional health. Studies have found that older people who are socially engaged and who maintain or increase their level of social activity have a slower progression of health decline than their peers who become more socially isolated.[86] Pascal agrees here as he says:

'I have watched friends deteriorate after retirement by being too self-attentive. We have been appalled by the way in which some friends in their seventies are shrinking into themselves. They are withdrawing from active involvement in community activities even when they have tons of time. Some are shrivelling into not much more than grandparents. Looking after grandchildren is something but NOT ENOUGH, we shriek! Too many of them are working on a model of having so much energy and that energy seems to be shrinking as they age. And this for baby boomers who have enjoyed a pretty lucky existence but now see no need to give to community even though they have all the time in the world.'

Pascal finds time to actively engage in his church community, in a church group for couples, on the board of a local museum, as a trustee of the National Railway Museum, a member of a local political party and an active member of his local choir!

Some health benefits of being socially connected are reduced risks of many health issues, including Alzheimer's disease, cardiovascular problems, arthritis and osteoporosis. Yvonne, 74, did not waste much time when her GP gave an early diagnosis of osteoporosis a few years ago; she got active! Yvonne now goes daily to the gym, is an active member of a weekly walking group and volunteers at a community garden. Locally, she cycles to her friends' places, her activities and to the shops, and this is just for her physical health. For fun and social interaction, she is a member of a card and knitting club and the local Friendship Force circle that meets regularly at the local farmers market for a coffee or a meal. Yvonne is a shining example to us all and leaves me in her wake with all her physical, social and volunteering activities. Healthy social connections can boost your immune system, lower blood pressure and improve your eating habits (eating is a very social activity, and social activities such as gardening reap edible rewards!). Social interaction with others can lead to a sharper mind, as well as giving you a sense of belonging.

The Importance of Social Connections

Research undertaken by the Centre for Social Impact has shown that 'the best conditions for making connections are where connection is a by-product, not the focus, of activities'. The research authors add: 'Working with social enterprises, we've seen that connection occurs where there is space and time to test out people's shared characteristics and build trust.'[87]

This is certainly something I have witnessed in conducting the conversation series. At the beginning of a ten-week program you start with a group of people where the majority do not know each other. As the weeks progress and trust builds up, it is wonderful to witness the connections that happen. Support is offered and friendships are formed. On several occasions, I have noticed that contact details have been exchanged and group members continue their connection and conversations well after the program has been completed. Recently I was invited to an afternoon tea with members of an earlier group. This group meets socially every few months (pandemic regulations permitting) and have formed an informal and supportive social friendship circle. On this occasion, after checking in with each other and some social chit-chat, all engaged in a healthy and robust discussion around the pros and cons of CPR at the end of life. Ongoing connection is a positive by-product of these conversation series!

As mentioned, studies show that social connections are important to our health and wellbeing as we age, and it is the quality of these social connections that is most important to health. Close, strong social relationships that are supportive, encouraging and meaningful are most beneficial. The broader, more superficial relationships are also important, because they provide the feelings of connectedness, familiarity and sense of self-worth that are associated with your position and role within your community.

Activity: Your social connections

Here's an activity from Pearson and Wilson that can help you visualise your social connections.[88] You will need a large piece of drawing paper (for this you can tape two A4 pieces of paper together), a collection of small items like pebbles, shells, coins and buttons, colouring pencils or crayons, and your journal and pen. Finding the small items may take a bit of time but it is worth doing. Otherwise, use a different coloured crayon for the different people in your life. When I work with a group of people, we use all sorts of small symbols, and each participant will find a figurine, symbol or item that signifies them and then find other items or symbols to represent their social connections.

When you have everything ready:

1. On a large piece of paper draw a circle which fills most of the paper. Write a title for the exercise, for example 'My social connections', 'My life'.

    Place a dot at the centre and write beside it 'Me'.

    If you are comfortable, close your eyes for a moment. Take a full slow breath and relax as you let it out. Relax your body, letting go of as much tension as you can.

    Then open your mind to a picture of your circle of friends, family and other social connections. See what comes to mind and take a few moments to see them clearly in your mind.

2. From your collection of pebbles, buttons and symbols find one item that represents you and place it in the centre. Is there anything you would like to say about what shape or colour you have chosen? Write your reflections in your journal or notebook.

3. Then think about your family, circle of friends and connections. Who are they? Find a pebble or button which represents each person or a group of people. Arrange these items on your page inside or outside the circle. Write the name of each person next to the item that represents them.

The Importance of Social Connections

4. When you've completed placing the items around your sheet of paper and naming them all, start adding lines that show the connections between people. The lines could be strong, weak, dotted, straight or curving. Use different colours to represent differences in the strength of connections, or how much effort you need to put into maintaining each connection.
5. Once you have done this, look at the web of relationships before you and consider the following questions. Record the answers in your journal for later reflection.
   - How close or distant from you is each person?
   - How do they connect with each other? Which ones are close, which are distant?
   - How do these connections get on with you and with each other?
   - Are they facing, or turned away from you? From each other?
   - Which ones would be closest to the centre and which closest to the edge? Is the distance important?
   - Are they inside or outside the circle?
   - Record something about how you arranged the figures.
   - Is there anyone significant in your life who is not on this page?
   - Who in your social connections circle are the people you feel nurtured by?
   - Conversely, it there anyone in your existing social circle whom you find draining or simply 'hard work'?
6. Next we are going to consider the question: Is this how you would like your social connections to be?
   - Consider possible changes to those you connect with and how you connect.
   - If this is not what you want, how would you really want it to be?
   - Are there any changes you would like to make? Could you show them? And if so, write down how it would be, how it feels.

To integrate all the work you have done on your circle of connections, you can record it by writing a brief description of your social connections and any other insights you gained from this exercise.

Social connections and the coronavirus pandemic

The coronavirus pandemic that started in Australia in 2020, and the enforced social isolation and social distancing it has generated (and continues to generate), has had a profound impact on the health and wellbeing of us all, particularly our older population. The social isolation and continued social distancing are major risk factors for mental and physical health, and their influence will be experienced for years to come. As I mentioned when discussing ageism, it is important to always consider the needs and human rights of older people and in a time such as we are experiencing now, it is even more necessary. 'To get through this pandemic together,' said Secretary-General of the United Nations Antonio Guterres, 'we need a surge in global and national solidarity and the contributions of all members of society, including older people.'[89]

When we are in lockdown, physical activities are limited and social engagements are not possible or are severely restrained other than via phone or internet technology. That is ok if you are able to afford the technology and internet access, are 'connected' and able to use it, but this is not always the case. Many Australian families are living apart, spread far and wide across the country, and regular visits when some live interstate or overseas are not an option. I am so thankful for technology as it enabled us to remain connected with our son, his wife and our grandchildren who live in Melbourne. If it were not for internet technology, we would have missed all our grandson's milestones of crawling, eating solids, walking, talking and play activities, and the first days and weeks of his new-born baby sister's life! How different this 'active and live' form of social connecting is compared with the connection I had with my family when I immigrated to Australia 40 odd years ago! We wrote our regular letters and made a phone call on birthdays. Even my mother at the age of 98 said: 'If only we had this technology when you left for Australia all those years ago!'

No matter what stage of our lives we are at, we can certainly see the positive impacts of neighbourly help and support, looking out for one another, and finding ways to connect with loved ones, friends or neighbours over the fence. As neighbours and citizens, we need to be inclusive and encourage everyone to look out for people in our communities and to strengthen and enliven our community networks. We need to practice what we preach, so that we are an integral part of the web of connections that we ourselves rely on. In Merily's words:

> 'In this era of Covid restrictions and semi-isolation the comfort and support that is received from friends has highlighted the dependence I have on the friendships of close friends. Loneliness which we are told is quite prevalent in many older people's lives must be most disabling. A kind comment, a concerned phone call and a desire to catch up can sustain the spirits over tough times. My close friends (all women) are tremendously important and valued for the laughter and intimacy they provide in a framework of trust and constancy. We all matter.'

What helps us, what helps *you* as an individual, to stay well connected? At the initial outbreak of the pandemic in 2020 and in full lockdown, I contacted Jacki several times via phone or letter to say hello and to check in. When I asked via email how she was getting on living alone during lockdown, Jacki told me in her reply about her spontaneous poetry writing. She attached the following poem:

Two chairs in my living room

I sat in my chair and looked across the room,
My cross-room chair looked back at me.
I said to that chair, 'I'm glad you're here.

A tantrum is coming, I sadly fear.'
It's no fun tantruming by myself.
My cross-room chair looked back at me,
In silence it gazed placidly.
I heard it say without a word
'I am here for you my dear.
Flying cushions, I accept,
My arms are soft and welcome fear.
I will witness all your woe
When outside you cannot go.
Turn me round and lean on me,
I am strong as you will see.
Come and talk to me for free
And look across the room.
Gaze upon your other chair
The one upon which you now do sit
It too will share your current shits.'
Exformation is the key,
Let it loose and you will see
Letting go will set you free.

JF, 2020

Companion animals such as a dog or cat play an important role in allaying loneliness and social isolation for many people. Delia mentioned how Harry, her parent's dog, is a great ongoing social companion for her father Archie who, since the death of his wife Daisy, lives alone. It is Harry who instigates many social connections in the neighbourhood. Archie lives across the road from the beach and on most days they go for a walk along the beach where they meet other dogs and their owners. Pets can be great social connectors, the presence of a dog regularly triggers conversation. Shandy is 65 and living on her own; she has experienced

The Importance of Social Connections

loneliness but mentions that her two dogs are great companions. Shandy also finds that her dogs are often the ones who instigate a greeting or chat with anyone they meet in the local neighbourhood or while on an outing to the park or the beach.

Even if your pet is one that you do not take for a walk, it can still be a valued companion. Sometimes it is the very presence of another living creature interacting with us that helps us feel better. And caring for a pet can help us feel useful, encourage us to make plans and be aware of the needs of another creature.

The honesty we bring to *this* conversation may sometimes cause us a little discomfort, especially when acknowledging that many of us recognise unhelpful or even harmful social connections that cause tension and distress, like ones you may have identified in the connections circle activity. Such a relationship could be with someone—even a family member—who is unkind or critical, who is full of self-talk but rarely listens or who provokes feelings of inadequacy. How can you manage this? The Greater Good Science Center published an article about how to cope with unhelpful relationships and put forward the five suggestions below,[90] to which I've added some extra thoughts.

1. 'Accept that you are in a difficult situation, dealing with a very difficult relationship.' Acceptance is a choice and likely more helpful than engaging in similar unkind behaviour because that does not help you to feel better about yourself and it does nothing to improve the situation.
2. 'The person will probably tell you that you are the cause of all their bad feelings.' You do not need to take this on board, you are not responsible for how they are feeling—that is *their* responsibility.
3. 'Tell the truth.' Remain open and honest in your conversations with people whose company makes you feel uncomfortable. This will take courage.

4. 'If you feel angry or afraid, bring your attention to your breath and do not speak (or write) to the person until you feel calm.' Wise advice as you may say or write something in the heat of the moment which you may regret later!
5. 'Have mercy.' Be kind and willing to forgive the other person and yourself. Accept the things you cannot change and keep yourself safe by stepping away where possible from harmful relationships.

What do we need to do or what *can* we do to make important changes? Healthy relationships and good social connections matter to all of us.

Activity

Reflecting on your social connections and how you intend to flourish till the end of your life, read through the following questions and record your answers in your journal.

- What do you need to consider on a personal level that helps you as an individual to stay well connected with others?
- What is important to you in your social relationships?
- What do you do to create and maintain social relations?
- Are there barriers to staying socially connected and, if so, what are they?
- Where do you socialise and how often?
- Cooking and eating are highly social activities, do you prefer to cook and eat alone or together with others?
- Consider your close, strong social relationships and the benefits you derive from these connections. What stands out, and why?
- How do you manage social relationships which are unhelpful or even harmful?
- Consider your broader, important but somewhat more superficial relationships. What and where are these connections and what do you enjoy about them?

- What can you do to build and enrich social connections in your community?
- What is the relationship between community and a high quality of life for you?
- Are your neighbours important?
- How do your living arrangements affect all of this and therefore your quality of life?

'Three good things' exercise

Each day for a week, write down three good things that happened. Is there a pattern? What things have made you happy?

'Flourishing or ageing well' exercise

Think about what matters to you most in life, then ask yourself what you can do to help yourself feel connected to it. Write a short story or a poem, or make a drawing, painting or collage representing the things that you enjoy doing, that make you flourish or feel happy or well.

Looking at the bigger picture

On a personal level we need to consider the questions, dilemmas and solutions we have discussed so far; however, healthy social connections are also an important issue for all levels of government. At all levels we need to consider which are the wide-ranging initiatives to socially engage people of all ages and differing abilities, the varied citizens of our communities. Our local governments and local businesses in partnership with other community sectors need to create communities which enable their citizens to stay active and socially connected. There are numerous things we need and must consider in creating functional and socially engaging environmental and urban designs of our neighbourhoods, towns, and cities. These actions benefit not only older people in the community, but help build a dynamic, caring and stable community that benefits all who live in it.

Wildevuur et al. in their book *Connect: Design for an emphatic society* highlight the following design principles for social connectedness: 'The designs:

- are empathetic, they put people and their context first
- facilitate encounters between people
- create space for narrative and action
- offer a positive experience
- remain open and transparent'.[91]

How do we design our neighbourhoods and communities so they enable independence while also providing the opportunity and ease for connection with others?

Governments tend to invest in bricks and mortar: building, renovations and restructuring to boost the building industry and our economy, as we saw in the building stimulus package the Australian Federal Government developed in 2020 during the Covid-19 pandemic. But is this just to boost the industry and economy, or will it also benefit those in need of housing or who want safer, liveable and more socially connected communities? The recent housing developments in the town where I live seem to be rather ad hoc, with little or tokenistic attention being paid to making them safe, healthy, socially durable and sustainable. How do we design for a vibrant, sustainable and socially connected community? And what can *we* do and need to do to make this happen? It requires the power of active citizens who encourage social participation on a large scale to transform community and create healthy social capital!

I will finish this chapter by telling you a good neighbourhood story. It is about Hulbert Street, in a Fremantle suburb, where Shani Graham and her partner Tim Darby live. Shani and Tim did not know their neighbours very well and felt a bit isolated in suburban life. Together they helped to lead a sustainable-living revolution that ultimately resulted in strong neighbourly relationships and the building of lasting community. Shani tells her story, 'Take a street and build a community', in a TEDx talk.[92] It is inspiring. Shani and Tim went on to set up an organisation,

The Importance of Social Connections

Ecoburbia, which is designed to create more sustainable, connected and resilient communities. In the short vimeo clip on the Ecoburbia website,[93] Shani speaks about the house where she and Tim live. This double house in suburbia has been divided into four spacious private apartments where other people are living, and together they share living space and a beautiful garden. This is an alternative and exciting form of housing to encourage social engagement and prevents loneliness. I will tell you more about this housing concept in the next chapter as it is a form of housing that offers many benefits for people over 65.

CHAPTER 7

Emerging and Established Housing Models

Home is where the heart is.
— PROVERB

Are you thinking about your current and future housing in relation to growing old? The house you live in impacts the way you experience living life in your later years. A house, the place we live, is more than bricks and mortar, it is usually the place we call home. It is a place where we feel safe and can be fully ourselves. It is a place where we have control and influence over the things that happen and the freedom to invite who we like and manage what and when we do things. Our house is our window and link into our street, neighbourhood and community; it holds our possession, things that make life more comfortable for us, and it plays a part in giving us that sense of belonging. It is or can be the place where we feel supported, socially and emotionally, to live life on our own terms. Hopefully, our house and our community environment will meet our basic needs and enables us to truly age well and in place.

The facts: The Australian Bureau of Statistics reported in 2016 that 71 per cent of older people owned their own home outright, 9.5 per cent still had a mortgage and the remaining 18.6 per cent rented their homes.[94]

Of further interest is that, in 2016, 26.8 per cent of older Australians lived alone, and of those there were more older women living alone.[95] Sadly, there is an increasing number of women over 55 experiencing housing pressure, uncertainty and homelessness.[96] These facts highlight how money matters in ageing: there are fewer people with the security of owning their home outright, while more still carry mortgage debt or contend with ongoing rental costs. A safe and secure home is not a given for all older people, which is shocking given that secure housing is a key indicator for ageing well, physically and emotionally.[97] Housing security is challenging for older people who live in private rental because they are subject to regular rent increases. One of the many worrying side effects of the Covid pandemic is the dramatic and unexpected rise in the cost of housing and, subsequently, private rental. Add to this the real prospect of eviction brought about by loss of work and income, and housing insecurity looms even larger for many older people. Further, there are waiting list for public housing in Australia, the length of the wait depending upon location and need. In some places, waiting times vary between 3 months for people in extreme need, to more than 5 years.[98]

According to an article in *The Conversation*, many older people think and worry about how and where they will grow old, and what choices they have in living in a suitable home and environment where the positives outweigh the negatives.[99] In my opening words at the beginning of this book, I wrote that most of us wish to live and die in our own home. Consider the benefits and the challenges: Is the house you live in suitable with the likely changes of health and mobility as you age—including end of life care? Do you need to consider change?

In chapter 4 Money Matters we discussed the cost of adapting our homes to enable us to age in place, and we've briefly mentioned downsizing. Maybe the harder question to consider is: why would you need to change where you live? Yes, it is hard to consider a time in the future when your mobility is reduced, or you need formal care to remain living in your own home. As with so many aspects of ageing, and despite the discomfort or reluctance, there are many reasons to start thinking about this now. Here are a few points for you to consider; make some notes in your journal as you do:

- Your house and garden are now too big for you to maintain and look after since your children have left home.
- Your house is over two or more levels, and stairs are becoming a problem.
- You are finding that access to the toilet and bathroom is becoming harder as your mobility changes.
- You are living on your own and the cost of your house causes financial pressure.
- You live alone and you are feeling lonely and socially isolated.
- You initially chose to live where you are because of work or children living nearby, but as things change this may not be the place you prefer to live now.
- You live in a city and you wish to live somewhere more rural or closer to nature.
- You live in a rural community with no medical centre and inefficient public transport.
- You have to give up driving, and it becomes difficult to get to the library, sports club, photography class.
- You would like to live in a neighbourhood or community where you engage with others in activities you like or to have more social connections with your neighbours.
- You would like to … (fill in your likes, needs and wants around housing).

Ageing in place may be our choice, but it is not always the ideal choice that it may initially appear to be. Honestly, we should also consider 'what place' when we think of ageing in place. Our houses need to be suitable for taking our ageing needs into consideration, but—as we've already noted—very few houses will have been designed with this in mind. A good, well designed and accessible house enables most people to remain safe and independent in all their day-to-day personal care and activities. However, many of us do not live in such places and modifications may be structurally challenging or financially unaffordable for many, particularly those living on a fixed budget. And for people in the private rental market, such changes may simply not be an option. Housing commission or housing trust tenants may be able to negotiate for assistance; it is worth checking what you may be entitled to.

In a rural environment or even in a typical suburb our cars are an important extension to our homes as being able to drive to various daily activities is a necessity. However, what happens when we can no longer drive? Are the footpaths in your suburb even and easy to walk on, and free from overhanging tree branches, for example? Could you use a mobility scooter on the footpath, or is it too narrow? Is there even a footpath? Check 'Road rules for wheelchair users' about the use of mobility scooters and electric wheelchairs on Australian roads. The Automobility website provide links to the regulations in each State and Territory and it provides tips for staying safe in your mobility device.[100]

In short, do you need to change your living and housing situation?

I have considered the above question seriously for several years as it is also my wish to live and die in my own home. Is my home environment suitable to age in place? At present: no, it is not—but it has possibilities. I live with my husband in a generous two-storey house, which is wonderful as we often have visitors and house guests. While we are still well, healthy, and active that is ok, but it is becoming too big for just the two of us and some areas are not very functional. For example, our main bathroom on the ground floor next to our bedroom has a huge bathtub (1800 mm long, 1150 mm wide and 500 mm deep) and yes, as I wrote in Money Matters: the shower is over the bath! This is how athletic I need to be for my daily shower: step onto a 300 millimetre high step, step over the next 280 millimetre high step into the bath, down into the 500 millimetre deep bath, and in undertaking this feat there is nothing much to hang on to! The 'wall' on the other side of the bath is a glass window looking into an atrium. Clearly, that tub is an accident waiting to happen, and it has got to go! Bathrooms are one of the most dangerous areas of a home.[101] It is time for me to get into action and renovate to a more universal and age-friendly design for our continued independent living. The bath will go and instead we will have a level, walk-in shower alcove. There will be safety features such as non-slip flooring, fold-down seat and a grabrail in place.

Our house is built on what was, up to a few years ago, two acres of land. As we reached our sixties we realised we needed to make our own future ageing plans, and maintaining a large garden was not part of it. After much thought and discussion we have subdivided our land and are building a co-housing community—I will tell you more about that later in this chapter. Further, sometime in the future, there is an option to divide our double-story house. One side could be suitable for a small family, and for us on the other side, a smaller two-bedroom apartment on the lower floor. This enables a further option of a small studio apartment on the upper floor. Renovating and creating a smaller home within our house is our take on downsizing. This future subdivision of our home enables both or one of us to move into the smaller apartment while still staying within our community and neighbourhood. We no longer have a need for a large family house, so that effectively means we downsize our living space, which will be more manageable for upkeep and maintenance, and we provide accommodation for another family, and a live-in carer in the studio apartment, if needed. It is our approach to finding creative solutions within our existing environment.

After her significant fall, and during the hospitalisation and recovery period, Jacki explored her options for a safer and more manageable home environment. Her intention was—and still is—to age in place and she therefore set about fully renovating and retrofitting her house and garden. Jacki thought this through and has done an impressive job of making sure her house and garden are safe and well designed. These home and garden modifications will support Jacki to live and die in her own home, which is in the friendly neighbourhood she knows so well and wants to live in.

My own considerations around our home and its suitability for our future ageing and Jacki's deliberations and implementations are what is called 'right-sizing'. Right-sizing means to explore size and liveability, and consider risks and possible hazards of the house and garden we are living in or a house we would like to move into. Right-sizing, according to Kathy Gottberg, 'is the conscious choice to create a life and lifestyle that more sustainably aligns with your unique self in the best possible way at every stage'.[102] Right-sizing means living in or modifying a house to ensure it perfectly meets your needs.

In reflecting on housing needs, we need to consider the living environment, the neighbourhood, and the community. Questions we might consider include: Is our right-sized house in close proximity to or within walking distance of shops, medical centre and social and other activities? Is it near efficient and affordable public transport? By exploring all options we gain an understanding of what type of house and environment will help us to age well, and what will support us in our decision making to remain living independently for as long as possible.

An ideal form of housing design, with respect to its built form, is universal design. According to the Centre for Excellence in Universal Design, 'Universal Design is the design and composition of an environment so it can be accessed, understood and used to the greatest extent possible by all people regardless of their age, size, ability or disability.'[103] A universally designed house and environment meets the needs for people of all ages and abilities, and required modifications are easy to implement.

The traditional western way of living has been more solitary and in self-contained housing: your own home and perhaps garden for you alone, or for you and your family. As we have seen in ABS statistics, there is now an increase in the number of people living alone and, according to a review undertaken by the SA Government Department of Wellbeing and Ageing, this is in part due to a large proportion of our population getting older as there is at the same time an increase in the number of younger and middle-aged people living on their own.[104] Some people choose to live alone and enjoy the solitude and their own company. Other people end up living alone, but not by choice. The loss of a partner or close friend due to illness, death, separation or divorce can leave you living on your own, and can also be a substantial risk factor for loneliness. And the loss of mobility or a lack of transport contribute further risks of you becoming disconnected from your community and developing social isolation and loneliness.[105]

A literature review undertaken by the Institute for Sustainable Futures found that there is a heightened interest by older people to downsize and to consider alternative housing models that will enable them to age well while also remaining socially connected within community.[106] Merily's comments echo this:

> 'My partner and I are now taking steps to build a small home, in advance, in a small community group where there is an ethos expressed of looking out for each other. This is not an old people cluster, but it will have a mixture of ages. We are not ready yet to move as our activities encompass many aspects of our home but knowing if one of us was to die there is a welcoming downsizing option and that is comforting.'

The above-mentioned review by the Institute for Sustainable Futures also found that baby boomers reportedly wish to live with or close to others, their existing networks and within intergenerational communities so they are not restricted to communities of people within their own age group.[107] Ageing in place is our choice and, as we have found, it is also a necessity. What used to be an 'old-aged people's home' has now become a residential care facility, which is a housing or care option only for people with significant physical or cognitive decline. If you do not qualify for a place in residential care (as determined by an Aged Care

Assessment Team assessment, see chapter five), or do not wish to move into residential care, you will need to remain living independently even though you may be frail and have increasing need for more support. Living close to or together with others can be a solution. Shared housing is an option and has its benefits: the social aspects and the option of collaboration with others, a sense of safety and security, shared support for each other and housing affordability. Good housing is considered to be a social determinant of health.[108] And from a personal and a public policy perspective, the preventative health value of shared housing/co-housing cannot be underestimated (pers. comm., Maria Brenton, founding member of Older Women's Co-Housing and UK Cohousing Network's Senior Cohousing Ambassador, 2019).

Before I share with you some of the alternative housing options for older people I invite you to consider some essential questions, and make some notes in your journal:

- How healthy and safe is the house you are living in?
- What would you like to change in your current housing and living situation?
- How at 'home' do you feel in your house and community?
- What would you like to do together with others?
- What would you look for when spending time with others—social connection, friendship, shared interests, shared values, beliefs?
- How do you envisage sharing a house or some living space with others?
- What would be your ideal guidelines to make this shared living situation suitable for all—what are you willing to 'give' and 'receive'?
- If you are willing to share a house in a situation such as our small co-development option, what are the deal breakers—what would you be willing to live with, and what would you categorically not

be willing to do? For example, share a laundry? Share cooking or gardening? Carpool?

What housing options do we currently have available?

Retirement and lifestyle villages

In Australia there are both private ownership and rental opportunities to choose from in retirement living. A retirement village or lifestyle village is an independent living housing complex with specifically designed living spaces for the older person. When care assistance is required internal or outside home-care agencies can provide support. Most retirement or lifestyle villages have common shared spaces where activities, socialising opportunities and meals are offered. While both retirement and lifestyle villages tend to offer similar housing options and services, the difference between them lies in the legal and financial structures of the village, and this varies under each State and Territory legislation. It is therefore imperative that you do your homework when making a choice, so you are fully aware of your own and the operator's rights and responsibilities. The contracts, funding models and expectations can vary widely. Get professional legal and financial advice if needed regarding the legal structures and financial costs to ensure you understand what you are signing up for when moving into a retirement or lifestyle village.

Retirement and lifestyle villages have their pros and cons. For some older people, they provide a sense of safety and protection, and feelings of social isolation may be reduced by having close connections with peers. The houses are designed for an older population, which enables independence for longer through ease of access in design and location (some are located close to local shops, community facilities and medical centres—but not all). Living in a retirement or lifestyle village may be more convenient for you and reduce stress about keeping up with home or garden maintenance.

For others, a retirement or lifestyle village is not a choice. They may be constrained by the costs or the legal contracts, or villages may not be their chosen lifestyle—just not the place they feel they belong or can call home. I know residents of a nearby retirement village who thoroughly enjoy living there; it is close to shops, restaurants and other community facilities and they appreciate living with other retirees. For Anne who also lives there, however, this is not the case. Anne does not enjoy living in 'this gated community'. It was not her choice, and she does not feel she belongs there. Anne has recently been diagnosed with depression, she shares with me her feeling of 'being lonely' and that her days 'are long with nothing much to do'. Deciding about whether to move into retirement living is an individual choice, we are all unique and we have our own way of being and living.

There are retirement or lifestyle villages that provide 'assisted living', meaning that you live in your own small, private apartment which has (most likely) a living room, bedroom, bathroom and small kitchenette, but you also have access to services such as a prepared main meal, personal care, cleaning support, emergency call systems and all the other activities and transport options that are available within the village. This kind of living provides extra support for people with advancing disabilities to continue independent living.

Some retirement or lifestyle villages offer more services and facilities, and the accommodation may consist of two or three bedroom houses with two bathrooms, garages and small gardens or courtyards. Facilities may run to swimming pools, gyms, tennis courts or bowling greens. They may be situated in prestige locations.

A retirement or lifestyle village sometimes seems to be the only option for a smaller house that is designed to meet the needs of an older person—especially if you wish to remain in a particular locality—as, traditionally, Australians have not built smaller houses and units. Some people are happy with what is offered in some of the villages but for others this is not what they are looking or hoping for. If you are considering a move to a retirement or lifestyle village, make sure you are clear on what the differences are and what is on offer before you make any decisions. As mentioned in our discussion on money matters, be aware when moving into a retirement or lifestyle village that you understand the sale or lease agreement and your obligations and costs when you move in, during your tenancy, and when you exit. To gain an understanding check out the Retirement Village Act in each State or Territory. Aged and Community Services has published a Retirement Villages fact sheet which has helpful information, and further information is available from The Retirement Living Council. The details for these organisations you will find under Resources at the end of this chapter. I would encourage you to explore all future housing options, do your homework, research the information, and find out all the facts before you make your final decision as this is part of maintaining your independence as you age.

Residential aged care

This is for older people who can no longer live independently at home, a situation that may arise due to advanced cognitive or physical decline. This option includes accommodation, normally in a private room, and general health and nursing care for 24 hours a day. To be approved as a resident to live in a government-funded residential care home you must be approved by an Aged Care Assessment Team (ACAT). Residential care is not really part of this conversation, although it would be important for you and your family to be familiar with local residential facilities and the services they provide, so that if or when the time comes that you need full-time care you will be in a position to make informed decisions quickly.

I am not fond of the large residential care facilities we see built around Australia, and find them rather impersonal. All the rooms seem to look the same, hospital/institutional style, a hospital-style bed placed in the middle of the room, accessible bathroom and just enough space for your own comfy chair and a few personal belongings that you can place next to the television in the exact same wall cabinet as in every other room. This is not creative design, nor innovative; there is nothing personal and little the resident can do to personalise their space. I have often wondered, how can we as a society support our older citizens to age well and age in place; are there alternative housing options and what could they look like?

These wondering thoughts send me on a quest and I set off on a journey in 2019—mentally and physically. This study tour took me to the United States of America, Scotland, England and the Netherlands to explore alternative housing options for older people. I visited various intergenerational and senior co-housing communities, shared housing, and small neighbourhood community clusters as well as a couple of alternative housing options specifically designed for people living with dementia, such as 'The Hogeweyk' dementia village in the Netherlands, ... and I came back INSPIRED! There are so many inspirational and innovative alternative housing options out there!

As I stated in chapter 6, in reference to social connections, not only does it take a village to raise a child, there is now also an emerging movement around healthy ageing which says it takes a village to age well. And by this I do not necessarily mean a retirement or lifestyle village. In this context, by a village I mean a community, a neighbourhood where community members care about and look out for one another, a village where people connect, engage, and support older people, enabling them to have ongoing purpose and ability to flourish in later years.

Emerging alternative housing models

Are there choices? Yes, there are alternative housing models other than retirement or lifestyle villages. The following is an overview of some established and emerging housing models to enable ageing in place.

The 'granny flat' (rather an ageist term!) is a self-contained living area located on the grounds of, or attached to, a single-family home, popularly called the 'granny flat' as it is often used to accommodate ageing parents. In a country like the Netherlands, this form of housing is called a 'kangaroo house' and it accommodates an older family member or a family member living with a disability, enabling independent living with support nearby if needed. A kangaroo housing model is where two independent houses are connected, often by a shared entrance.

Enid's house is like that. She has a larger main house with an attached independent living space, and both are indeed connected by a shared entrance. Enid shared her story of living together with her daughter and young granddaughters, which occurred over three separate episodes of living together, lasting between a year and five years. Issues of family relations, including births, parenting and partnership break-ups, and a lack of communication caused problems, and Enid concluded by saying:

> 'I can't stress it too much, it is almost *all* about communication. We have become quite good to be very open about our needs and expectations and we still make mistakes. Life is constantly changing; we think we know each other's needs and we still get caught out. Forgiving and a willingness to keep trying is also very important. Living with the next two generations keeps me on my toes; it prevents me from getting into a rut. I quite like it and I know it's good for me. The grandchildren enjoy having another adult in their lives, and I enjoy their company. We help each other out when need be. Helping is a good example of how we try to do things here. The agreement is that we can always ask each other and if it is too much to ask, we have the option to say 'no' without offending each other.'

Pascal, as mentioned earlier, is not much of a forward planner but he did express being concerned around his and his partner's finances for their ageing future while still paying off their mortgage. On the topic of future housing he said:

'One possible scenario is that we move in with our second daughter and her husband. They may be able to buy a spacious house as they will receive financial support from the in-laws. We've considered co-investing as well with the aim of us having an annexe—granny flat—to live in.'

If you are contemplating building a granny flat (also called a habitable space) then you are required to comply with the Australian Building Code and local planning regulations to gain development approval and building certification, depending on government regulations. It is important to check this out, and it varies depending on State and local government regulations. Work out what you need to consider before moving into a granny flat. Will you be moving into a granny flat which is located on the property of an adult child or do you move out of your home into a granny flat and provide your child with a home option? Make sure you have a clearly written agreement in place and maybe seek support from a legal professional to help you with the drawing up of a legal document. This can prevent misunderstanding and conflict in the family when you die.

What you may wish to consider:
- financial contribution: rent, rates, utilities, maintenance
- maintenance responsibilities
- use of communal equipment: washing machine, dryer, tools or garden equipment
- involvement with or expected responsibilities in providing care for grandchildren.

Ask yourself:
- Will you be fully independent and have privacy in your space?
- What will happen when your health deteriorates and you need more care?
- How will this arrangement affect your relationship with your child and his/her family or with any of your other children?

- Are there other legal matters to consider when you move into a granny flat on a family member's property? For example, how will it affect your pension?

Make sure you have a clear, signed agreement in place between you and the owners of the home and land, and as I suggested earlier, seek legal advice before you commence building or move in.

Shared housing

More people are choosing to live together in one house, often without there being a family connection. Many people may remember the share houses of their youth, often with too many people and much coming and going. Rather than the transient nature of most of those youthful experiments in community, shared housing for older people can be more permanent and a richer experience. Each person has their own living space and together they share some common spaces. This can be a good balance between the benefits of social connection, shared activity, support and safety, and individual privacy. There are a few thriving examples here in Australia. 'The Shedders' are three couples in their sixties and seventies who as good friends bought some land and built a large house together where they could all retire and provide support to one another. See their story on the Collaborative Housing website.[109]

Another example is the AGEncy Project, a community of people who mostly live around Balmain in Sydney's inner west, who want to create a place where they can live actively and independently as they grow old. It is called The AGEncy Project because the people living there want to retain agency as they grow older. They want to contribute and be relevant to their community, maintaining control over their decisions and remaining engaged and active within their community. Read more about their plans on their website.[110]

Homeshare

This is an international movement, nearly 50 years old, that started in the United States and came to Australia more than 20 years ago. Basically, an older person with a spare room is matched up with a younger person who will provide some domestic help and companionship in exchange for free accommodation or reduced rent. In Australia and New Zealand, Homeshare Australia and New Zealand Alliance (HANZA) provides the professional expertise to match up 'older householders or householders with a disability who could benefit from help in the home and companionship, with people of integrity prepared to lend a hand in return for affordable accommodation'. The system has many benefits, both for the householder and the home sharer. Householders get to remain in their own home, receive practical assistance with domestic tasks and benefit from the safety of an overnight presence. Home sharers get relatively cheap, conveniently located, stable accommodation.[111] In addition, there is the bond of companionship and connection that can form between the two parties.

Rina, 70+, is an artist who, after the death of her husband and the loss of her home in a bushfire, rebuilt her house and studio where she continued to live on her own. Rina took part in a conversation series, Ageing Well in your Community, and shared with the group that she has a significant hearing impairment that has resulted in social isolation and loneliness. The group was supportive and new friendships were formed. Interestingly, one of these new friends connected Rina to a person in need of accommodation. The positive outcome of this connection led Rina to provide a bedroom and the shared facilities in exchange for some extra income and a welcome social connection.

The Henry Project

The Henry Project, named for American philosopher Henry Thoreau, is interested in assisting homeowners to modify their existing homes or to build new houses that will allow multiple households to live together under one roof. There would be independent private living spaces as well as shared communal areas. In addition, the Project has developed a street initiative to encourage people to make use of their verges, front yards or other under-used spaces to create community spaces. The focus of the Henry Project is 'the idea that the design of our housing should consider the social dimension of sustainable development ... to improve the wellbeing and quality of life of residents, neighbours, and communities by providing spaces that make it easy to find connection and to sustain that social connection in the long term.' For details see their website.[112]

Co-housing

Co-housing is an intentional community, with private houses of different designs and sizes clustered around shared spaces. Co-housing originated in Denmark in the early 1960 where it is called a living community.[113] American architects Kathy McCamant and Charles Durrett visited Denmark where they learned about these living communities and they in turn introduced this housing model in America and named it co-housing.[114] A modern version of co-housing is emerging throughout Australia, where homeowners are sharing communal spaces and facilities to reduce their environmental impact and household bills. Shared spaces include a shared common house with guestroom and activity space, community garden and parking spaces, and could include a shared laundry and work-shed. The design of a co-housing community encourages both individual, privately owned homes with social connection and contact through shared common facilities. Residents of a co-housing community generally have shared management and maintenance responsibilities. Co-housing is particularly well established in the Netherlands, Denmark and parts of the USA. Other western countries are seeing the benefits of co-housing and here in Australia there are now a number already established or in the process of being established. For further information on co-housing, see Co-housing Australia or check out co-housing in your state.[115]

Co-housing communities can be single generation or multigeneration. A multigenerational co-housing community includes people of all ages, a normal mixed society. Being connected to others is important for our physical and psychosocial wellbeing. We need strong ties with family, friends and our neighbours as they provide us with security, support, happiness and a sense of purpose and belonging.

These communities bring people together and are based on community members being good and supportive neighbours. This form of housing and community is appealing to active older people wishing to have a mix of young and old to enable engagement between people of all ages. Residents sharing occasional meals, activities and tasks build stronger and healthier communities where young and old support each other. The benefits for the younger and older residents are mutual as was highlighted in a recent report from Canada where their challenges of housing, social isolation and accessibility are not dissimilar to Australia.[116]

Senior co-housing specifically for people 60+

Senior co-housing functions the same as intergenerational co-housing, but here people over 60 are choosing the company of their peers. Even within senior co-housing you will find several generations living together, as the age of residents can be anything from 60 to 90+. Senior co-housing is specifically designed with accessibility, safety and supports in mind to meet the needs of older residents. It provides mutual support, opportunities to socialise and age in place. Some senior co-housing communities offer temporary accommodation for a caregiver who can be hired to live in when more professional or specialised care is required.

These co-housing communities, whether multigenerational or senior, enable the older person to be autonomous and active within community life where they have their privacy and play an active role in community and management—all of which gives meaning to life. There is plenty of information on co-housing on the internet and I recommend two books: *Creating Cohousing* by Kathryn McCamant and Charles Durrett and *Senior Cohousing* by Charles Durrett. During my visit study tour to the USA, I had the opportunity to meet with Charles Durrett and some other residents in the co-housing community where he lives.

There are numerous co-housing communities throughout Australia, but I promised earlier in this chapter to tell you about Miller's Corner Cohousing. As I mentioned in chapter one, my family and I moved from Sydney to rural South Australia in 1996. It was a difficult move as Sydney had become home and having moved 1000 kilometres to South Australia we as a family had that difficult task familiar to anyone who has made similar moves, to start all over again making new connections and friendships. When our children completed their education and started to leave home, friends asked us if we considered moving back to Sydney. That was not an option, we had moved too often, and we had made new and valuable connections here, it was time to call this place home. Our large house, initially on nearly 2 acres of land, is in the heart of what was twenty-five years ago a small rural township. Over the years, the ever-increasing population of this town has now made it a large regional centre within cooee of a capital city. It was memories of that re-location from Sydney and the need to feel we belonged somewhere that initiated thoughts about creating our own community.

Over the years the land was being developed around us. Next door, the estate of John Dunn, an early settler to the region, became a retirement village, and the four acres of land behind us that had been home to grazing sheep became a housing estate. The developers of both these projects wanted to purchase our land; we declined and decided we needed to develop it ourselves. So, over the last ten-plus years we have given deep thought and worked hard to create Miller's Corner, a multigenerational co-housing community.[117] Miller's Corner is designed to encourage both social contact and individual space. In our small village we will have nine private, energy-efficient homes clustered around a shared common house that we call Forest House, all interspersed with community gardens.

There is an extra block of land for us to build 'HomeHouse', a house which will be specifically designed for people over sixty, but more on that in a moment. We are now well into the building stages, and I am happy to report that our first three lots of residents have moved in. This village-like cluster is designed to meet the needs of children, adults including older adults and people living with a disability, so that all will be able to actively participate in the operation of their own neighbourhood.

The concept of HomeHouse—translation for ThuisHuis—comes from the Netherlands. A ThuisHuis is small-scale living for older people who live on their own and who are at risk of becoming socially isolated and lonely. ThuisHuis is a large, ordinary looking house located in an ordinary street. It has six individual private apartments where each resident has a small lounge/living space, bedroom, bathroom, and kitchenette behind their own private 'front' door, and together the six residents have an extra shared lounge activity space, a larger kitchen, and a guest room (which can also be used for a live-in carer). ThuisHuis in the Netherlands is connected to a group of volunteers who provide support and assistance to the residents with social activities and (re)connection within the wider community.[118]

At Miller's Corner we plan to build a ThuisHuis, a HomeHouse along similar lines to the Dutch model, a plan that is supported by residents living at Miller's Corner. I repeat, 'It takes a village to age well'. As we are an establishing community it is our intention to have as first residents of HomeHouse a mixed group of 'younger' active older 60+ people and people living with disability. This will enable all Miller's Corner residents, young and old, to engage and contribute towards building community, which puts us in good stead when we get older and are needing some extra neighbourly support. In a way, by building HomeHouse we will have senior co-housing within multigenerational co-housing at Miller's Corner! What makes Miller's Corner unique is that, as a co-housing community, we are within a few minutes' walking distance from the heart of our town: from shops, leisure activities, walking and cycling tracks, and nearby transport—for me, it is a place where I wish to be in my ageing future.

Cohousing for Ageing Well (CHAW) is an initiative by architect Damian Madigan, and is another local South Australian proposed model of housing.[119] This is a collaborative research project that is exploring how to retain, alter and extend existing homes and provide new small-scale housing, around shared gardens on the existing block of land, that are suitable for people of any age. It is funded by and a collaboration between various state organisations and local government councils.[120]

If indeed Australians wish to have a choice and make decisions about where they will age in place, what needs to change to support a choice in housing? According to Brodsky, Grey and Sinclair, the following areas are where change needs to be made, particularly in government policy:[121]

- transaction costs: for example, stamp duty, that discourage people from moving before it becomes essential, as it often does for the over-eighties
- disincentives to releasing equity in the family home: for example, the pension means tests on proceeds, in interaction with the pension and superannuation systems, can put people in a worse financial situation
- housing stock, styles of housing and location: there needs to be a greater variety on offer
- emerging home ownership models: for example, home equity release, reverse mortgages and cooperative housing, to name a few.

So, as well as improvements in choice of suitable housing, financial policy changes are needed. What are the long-term affordable housing and rental options for people with a low or very moderate financial status?

In addition, urban design and planning policies need to change. How do we keep older people in their own home and community? How can we make changes to urban planning policies to enable small-scale housing units on what once was a 'large' houseblock, as is proposed in the 'Cohousing for Ageing Well' project? What needs to happen to encourage emerging home ownership models such as the ones outlined above? Governments need to make changes to policies to enable older people to customise their homes as they age or to be able to downsize and move without being financially penalised.

If your wish is to age in place you may, like me, also need to consider retrofitting or renovating your home so it fully meets your needs for safety and wellbeing into the future. The most crucial consideration is to be pro-active and get these renovations done early. Prevention is better than cure. Consider these modifications as a safety measure not only for yourself but also for your ageing friends and others who visits your home.

Perhaps you are contemplating a move and, if so, have you explored the various options available and their associated costs. Have some courage and take the initiative to have a conversation with friends, peers or experts and ask for their opinions. Who knows where those conversations may lead, you may end up considering an inspiring, innovative shared housing model!

Although a shared mode of living is still not very common in Australia, it is gaining traction and can be a housing model which supports the health and wellbeing of older adults and also be of interest and benefit to our wider community. Take a moment to consider the pros and cons. Shared housing or co-housing is about choosing to live with others and working out how you can enjoy living together. Remember the story of the Shedders from earlier in the chapter? Co-housing may include designing a shared house in collaboration with others, working out your shared values and how to engage socially and make decisions together. Sharing a house or a community involves shared values, collaboration, shared responsibilities and mutual support. Shared housing requires adjustments, and it requires collaboration and negotiation with other residents and respecting each other's privacy. Yes, you may experience conflict and disagreements and other challenges that are part of community life. On the other hand, shared housing and co-housing communities offer autonomy, shared engagement in activities and decision making as well as social, emotional and practical support. Shared housing and co-housing communities create a sense of belonging and safety among the residents and alleviate social isolation and loneliness. Living with others can be an opportunity to experience an inspiring, and more connected, way of living—which is a huge health bonus. Together you choose to stay in charge of your own life. Requirements are an open mindset and a passion for living life.

Activity

Consider doing this activity on your own or in discussion with a circle of friends. Take turns to share your thoughts. Listen and learn from each other.

Regardless of how healthy you are right now, it is important to consider the longer-term advantages of living in or moving to a home where you will be more comfortable and safer as you grow older. By asking yourself these questions now, you are better positioned to make informed choices rather than being forced to make a pressured and rushed decision when a crisis arises.

Consider these questions about your house and community and record your thoughts in your journal:

- How 'at home' do I feel in my home?
- Is my home designed to have the flexibility to evolve over time as health and mobility change? Are modifications required?
- Does my house and garden require a lot of upkeep and maintenance that cuts into my budget and/or free time?
- Is my current home depleting my savings or causing me unwanted financial stress?
- To what extent do I feel I belong in my community? Would I be happier living closer to family and friends?

- Do I have easy access to services such as a medical centre, shops, leisure activities, walking and bike paths and nature parks?
- Does my neighbourhood have adequate public transport for the days that I would rather use public transport than drive, or for when I am no longer able to drive?
- What opportunities do I have where I live now to do the things I love to do?
- What cultural activities do I need close to a place I call home?
- What opportunities are available for me to express myself through work in the community? Where can I contribute with meaning and purpose?
- What are my thoughts about the various housing models described in this chapter: Do any of them appeal? What, from my point of view, are the positive or negative aspects of the various housing models?

Do not wait too long to change your housing situation if that is the conclusion you have come to. Make these changes while you are still capable of making the decisions yourself. Change requires courage and energy, but it is worth doing: after all, it is your future you are planning!

Resources

J. De Campo, K. Jones, L. McPhee & C. Vanstone. 2021. *The Future of Home*. The Australian Centre for Social Innovation. TACSI, Adelaide. https://tacsi.org.au/future-of-home/

The Retirement Living Council – Located under Property Council of Australia https://www.propertycouncil.com.au/Web/Membership/Divisions/RLC_Division/Web/Membership/RLCDivision/Welcome.aspx?Division=RLC&hkey=fc5730d4-57da-4187-b007-b9ad911c2ebf

Aged and Community Services Australia: a national peak body supporting not for profit, church and charitable providers of retirement living, community, home and residential care. https://

www.acsa.asn.au/ ACSA state contact details: Victoria: (03) 9108 0750; New South Wales: (02) 8754 0400; Queensland: (07) 3505 3760 Tasmania: (03) 6105 0246; South Australia / Northern Territory: (08) 8338 7111; Western Australia: (08) 9244 8233; Australian Capital Territory: (02) 6282 7827

C. Durrett. 2009. *The Senior Cohousing Handbook: A community approach to independent living.* New Society, Gabriola Island, BC, Canada.

K. McCamant & C. Durrett. 2011. *Creating Cohousing: Building sustainable communities.* New Society, Gabriola Island, BC, Canada.

C. Riedy, L. Wynne, M. Daly & K. McKenna. 2017. *Cohousing for Seniors: Literature review.* Prepared for NSW Department of Family and Community Service and Office of Environment and Heritage, by Institute for Sustainable Futures, University of Technology, Sydney.

K. Rusinovic, M. Van Bochove & J. Van de Sande. 2019. Senior co-housing in the Netherlands: Benefits and drawbacks for its residents. *International Journal of Environmental Research and Public Health.* Doi: https://www.mdpi.com/1660-4601/16/19/3776

Dementia specific village: 'The Hogeweyk' in the Netherlands. https://hogeweyk.dementiavillage.com

CHAPTER 8

Living Life with Meaning and Purpose

For this conversation we consider living with meaning and purpose in life. What do we have to offer the world? What is our 'work'? What do we still hope to achieve and what has been left undone? Considering this topic, the book *Tuesdays with Morrie* came to mind. This book, its subtitle 'An old man, a young man, and life's greatest lesson', is a true story about the author Mitch Albom's regular visits to his old sociology professor, Morrie Schwartz, who was dying of motor neuron disease. Their conversations became Morrie's last class: lessons in how to live.[122] I would highly recommend you read this book, a story of a wise elder and his student. Bill Plotkin in his book *Nature and the Human Soul* describes 'The Sage: Archetype of late elderhood' as ageing consciously, becoming an 'elder', a wise person, a peace maker and a person who is remembered positively, that is, leaves a legacy.[123] Another book that may also inspire you is *From Age-ing to Sage-ing* by Zalman Schachter-Shalomi and R.S. Miller. We all matter, each of us has something to contribute, in large or small measures and of equal importance.

Many of us are the 'younger old'; we are entering the third age, now considered by many to be the golden years, the time in our lives when we are likely to have fewer responsibilities and are able to experience more enjoyment of life.[124] If you are in good health, with or without financial resources, this time enables you to explore what it means to engage in life with purpose and meaning, and to make choices to do what you would want to do. You can take advantage of the many options available in learning something new, for example, further studies at university or the University of the Third Age, WEA courses, workshops and activities organised by local councils and community centres. You may have an interest in joining a local walking group, men's shed, sporting activities or a local choir, music group or friendship circle. Overall, when I look at my friends and others in their mid to late sixties and seventies, I see people exploring and being engaged in life and the world. Many in this age group describe the joys of undertaking activities that are not driven by work or employment needs or family-related responsibilities.

People in the third age are vibrant and active people, with a zest for life. When Greg retired from a job that had him working in various locations around Australia and overseas, he wanted to engage in an activity which was fun and which he could do with others. He learned to play the ukulele in a local community arts centre and by playing with others he has made new connections and formed some close friendships. For Greg this was enormously meaningful as due to all his travel and work commitments he had never had the time or ability to commit to attending group activities, clubs or a team sport on a regular basis. As part of a ukulele group, he engages in group lessons and concerts, and you can see him and fellow musicians at the local farmers market every Saturday morning. Greg thrives on this activity and he 'belongs' to the local musos. In all honesty, Greg was only 'retired' for a few years as he is now contributing to community by taking on a role as a community builder. Although he is in his late sixties, he is not concerned about forward planning to age well ... yet. He said that he will read my book when the time comes!

These can be the most positive, hence 'golden' years of your life. This is certainly my experience. Fortunately, I am healthy and active; I experience this stage in life as allowing more inner freedom and a lesser need to conform or to be accommodating. It is a time that permits me to be me and to explore who I am, to consider what I would still like to experience in life, and to discover where I can make a difference and contribute to the world around me. Pascal, as mentioned, is still employed and works on

> 'Trying to make a difference rather than achieving ... I am using my time to build a culture of collaboration in the tourism sector. I enjoy working where I can use my decades of experience to help people who are having a go and sometimes risk everything. I gain most inspiration from younger people—and their respect for me as a wiser, older person is confidence instilling. Equally, I look to people older than me who are still powering on, and that generates energy. I think especially of Pope Francis, lately also of President Biden, I am not too old to keep working at life, they tell me.'

Having said that, along with this vibrancy and zest for life in the younger old, there is also an acknowledgement and acceptance by this age group that we are getting older. There is no denying the experience of the physical decline of our bodies. By looking in the mirror, we see the wrinkles in our skin, the sagging body, the greying or disappearing hair; we notice the subtle aches in our knees, hips or back and the other physical ailments that can come with age, and which are unlikely to improve. The aches and pains you address to the best of your ability and there will come a time when you need to accept and learn to live with the discomforts of an ageing body. But even though we are growing older and eventually frailer, most of us would like to remain active, engaged and viable members of our communities and within society at large. As older people we still have a lot to offer and we wish to continue to live life with meaning and purpose. Living a good life that is meaningful and has purpose is also associated with better physical and psychological health, including for older people.

Victor Frankl, in his book *Man's Search for Meaning*, describes 'three possible sources for meaning: in work (doing something significant), in love (caring for another person), and in courage during difficult times'.[125] Hugh Mackay, well-known Australian social researcher, suggests that 'the meaning of life' is too hard to define and, instead, he writes about living a good life: 'a life which is characterised by goodness, a morally praiseworthy life, a life valuable in its impact on others, a life devoted to the common good'.[126] Living a meaningful and purposeful life requires an awareness of self, plus regular self-examination and self-reflection to gain a true understanding of who I am as a person.

People strive for meaning in their lives, through religion, other forms of spirituality, philosophy, meditation. Who am I, and how do I as a human engage lovingly with life and other people I meet on my life journey? Our purpose, our driving force in life, is to try to find, explore and achieve that sense of meaning; our purpose is to be concerned with giving as well as taking, of thinking kindly of others and acting kindly towards others as you would like them to think kindly about and behave towards you, supporting others as you would like to be supported. Living life with meaning and purpose includes others, it can be about caring and lovingly contributing to the wellbeing of humankind, 'the common good' and the natural world around us.

At this age of our lives, it becomes even more important to become aware of and talk about what gives life meaning as we also consider our purpose now and into the future. What is more, we do not have to wait. We can reset our focus on what is important to us, as an older person we would like to know that our life matters and where we can still contribute. Why am I here and what makes life worth living in the future? On what terms do I wish to live the remainder of my life? These are powerful questions to consider as we age. What life are you living now? Have you been true to yourself? Do you live a life that nourishes and stimulates you and expresses the very best of who you are? Allow yourself some time to ponder these questions—you may even do some writing in your journal.

If you have never done so, this is the time for some introspection and serious consideration about who you are now and who you want to be in the future.

These are not trivial issues to consider, and the answers may not come easily or be easy to face. While reflecting on these questions, it is likely that thoughts of regret will arise. Have I done ok? Have I done things that are good for others in my life? Could I have done things differently? And what did I learn from my mistakes, if anything?

I recently read an article about an Australian palliative care nurse, Bronnie Ware, who spent years looking after patients in the last three to twelve weeks of their lives, and this reading led me to her website.[127] Ware documented their epiphanies at end of life, in her book *The Top Five Regrets of the Dying*,[128] and was stunned to see the clarity and commonality between the thoughts they expressed. She shared some of the emotions people experience in their last stage of life and one of these was regret.

Most of us have regrets in our lives. Ware lists five common themes. In all honesty, the first regret Ware mentions—'I wish I'd had the courage to live a life true to myself, not the life others expected of me'[129]—particularly rattled me. It still has me wondering: am I courageous enough to live a life being true to myself? 'Yes', in some instances, but 'no' in others. No, I am not always courageous enough. I make compromises and know that conforming, fear and uncertainty around making some changes stand in the way. I know and am aware that we are not always able to do as we want or please, and know that I need to encourage myself to conform less, be clear on things that matter for me, and follow those aspirations.

I wonder, and here I speak from my own perspective, is being courageous around making changes about choice, about the choices we make around living our lives? Or is it related to being stuck in habits which are difficult to break? As part of writing this book I am reading literature on various topics. I recently read *A Biography of Loneliness* by Fay Bound Alberti. She writes:

We carry our individual experiences into the world and they shape us; we are also shaped by our engagements with others, and this bidirectional process is continual and ongoing. This is why we are emotionally embedded in the physical and environmental worlds in which we live throughout our lives and not merely in childhood. Like the million small rituals of our everyday lives, our emotional expectations and beliefs become internalized until they are as natural as breathing. Is this another reason why chronic loneliness is so hard to change? Embodied habits—from nail biting to overeating—are notoriously difficult to break; so, too, is getting out of negative mind sets.[130]

So, is this why I am in some parts of my life stuck in patterns that seem to prevent me from being true to myself, and find it difficult to make changes? Definitely food for thought and something I would like to have a conversation about with my peers.

I truly wish I could let myself relax, be happier and laugh more. Due to the Covid-19 enforced lockdowns in parts of Australia, our son, daughter-in-law and their 13-month-old son Felix came to live with us for over four months in 2020. With Felix's help I (re)gained that great and delightful sense of wonder, joy and delight of being a young child exploring the world, seeing the world as new through curious eyes and engaging in giggles and belly laughs. It was magical! We have five delightful grandchildren and their sense of joy and freedom in those early days of their lives is real happiness. They teach us how to be totally present, totally open to new experience, totally true to ourselves. Therefore, to help me be true to myself, I will explore my regrets and make peace with them. You too can think about any regrets that you may carry: reconcile them and, if it fits and you feel like it, have a giggle and good belly laugh on occasions.

Do you need to make amends for any of your regrets? With your journal beside you to record your thoughts, ask yourself where you can and need to make amends. Understand how any regrets came about, work out how to come to terms with them and move forward. Move on from regret and acknowledge your blessings: this encourages you to contribute to others, to give something back. Let a sense of purpose be your driving force; it is your motivator to make a positive impact on the world.

Work out what is important to *you*, write down the things or causes that you are passionate about. What motivates you and what makes you feel alive? Set some goals, short term as well as long term, specifically focused on your broader life purposes. With your goals in place, take small but purposeful steps. Life is a journey and so is purpose. Do you even know what your broader life purpose, wishes and goals currently are? Think about them now. Our purpose changes over our lifetime depending on where we are in life and what matters at the time. Like life, purpose evolves. Living a life of purpose gives both fulfilment and meaning to your journey. A wonderful activity which helps you to explore the above questions is the 'Tree of Life' from the book *Retelling the Stories of our Lives* by David Denborough.[131]

Tree of life

The roots—Write down where you come from here on the roots. This can be your home town, state, country, etc. You could also write down the culture you grew up in, a club or organisation that shaped your youth, or a parent/guardian.

The ground—Write down the things you choose to do on a weekly basis here. These should not be things you are forced to do, but rather things you have chosen to do for yourself.

The trunk—Write your skills and values here. I chose to write my values starting at the base of the trunk going up. I then transitioned into listing my skills. For me this felt like a natural progression from roots to values to skills.

The branches—Here write down your hopes, dreams, and wishes. These can be personal, communal, or general to all of humankind. Think both long and short term. Spread them around the various branches.

The leaves—Write down the names of those who are significant to you in a positive way, your friends, family, pets, heroes, etc.

The fruits—Write down the legacies that have been passed on to you. You can begin by looking at the names you just wrote on leaves and thinking about the impact they've had on you and what they've given to you over the years. This can be material, such as an inheritance, but most often this will be attributes such as courage, generosity, kindness, etc.

(Tip: if your tree is pretty crowded by this point, perhaps try drawing some baskets of fruit at the base of your tree and label them there.)

The flowers and seeds—Write down the legacies you wish to leave to others on the flowers and seeds.

(Tip: again, you may wish to de-clutter your drawing by visualising saplings, baskets of flowers, etc. on which to write these items.)

So far, I have mainly spoken about the 'early' years of ageing and having the ability to still be out and about and contribute to life and society in areas which matters to us as people. But how is meaning and purpose experienced by the frail 'older' old person, a person who due to increased frailty, psychological or physical illnesses is less able to actively take part in life? Meaning and purpose in life are in numerous ways linked to being connected to others. A Swedish study by Harrefors, Savenstedt and Axelsson found that 'a pervading fear of the healthy elderly was that they would lose their sense of identity and become "a nobody with no meaningful connections"'.[132] That is certainly how Anne experienced living in her retirement unit. 'There is just nothing to do here, and no-one needs me,' she exclaimed to me one day. Due to failing eyesight and increasing frailty Anne was not able to be as active or contribute as she had done previously. She had enjoyed gardening, cooking and socialising but in the retirement village much was done *for* her, not *with* her. Sadly, with the global pandemic, socialising was discouraged and social activities earlier provided for residents were stopped. Anne's daughter has a full-time job and does her best to support Anne where needed. Anne did not qualify for home help services as she managed these tasks still somewhat independently or with the support from her daughter. I believe (from an occupational therapy perspective) that Anne would have benefitted from some help in her residential care unit—not to do for her but with her, and to give Anne a new regular social connection. This would have also given her some agency, because the household chores were something she would still have been capable of managing and it would therefore have contributed to her sense of having a purpose and meaning in her life.

As my mother in The Netherlands aged, she did receive home help services for several years. The support person was always the same person; they connected, formed a bond and the two of them got on fabulously well together. Bea would come every two weeks for 2.5 hours and the two women would work together. Bea allowed Mum to be in charge and would always ask: What needs to be done? and where would you like me to start? Mum had the tasks of washing the breakfast dishes and cleaning the kitchen sink and bench tops while Bea cleaned the oven and mopped the floor. When Bea cleaned the bathroom, she organised Mum to do some light ironing, or Mum would do the dusting while Bea vacuumed the floor. Where possible they worked together as a team and this while Mum was aged in her eighties to well into her late nineties. Come 10.30 am they would both stop, sit down together, and enjoy some chitchat over morning tea. The work got done, Mum contributed and felt in charge and they enjoyed social conversation together. It was for both a very meaningful arrangement. This simple engagement of home help services provided in a person-centred manner ticked so many positive and healthy boxes of living with meaning and purpose and having good social connection. If Anne had received this type of support services it could have offered a meaningful connection, purpose and self-efficacy.

In our frailer years, either living at home or in residential care, we still want to contribute and know that we matter. We like to be seen and acknowledged, be heard, and taken seriously. Many a tragic story about elder abuse and neglect was told at the Royal Commission into Aged Care Quality and Safety conducted in 2019 and 2020. The stories clearly reveal that the older person was not respected, cared for, or acknowledged for who they were at that stage in their life.[133] I am sad to report that Anne has now been moved to a residential care facility with full-time care. Her loneliness turned into depression and further health decline. She is now even more dependent on others—well cared for but with nothing to do. I hope that there are resources and caring staff to engage Anne and that she is not seen as 'just another resident' to be cared for. Let there be engaged and willing staff, and resources (including time) to involve each person in meaningful activity and conversation, for staff to have time to connect and 'be present' with each resident instead of—as I have personally witnessed—talking over the resident's head about their own personal social lives with colleagues.

Can we, as frail older people, as we reflect on our life lived, accept and appreciate all we have achieved as well as reconcile some of our failures and disappointments? Do we have a better sense of who we are and how we made a difference in our lives? Frankl makes an important point that is worth contemplating:

> It is true that the old have no opportunities, no possibilities in the future. But they have more than that. Instead of possibilities in the future, they have realities in the past—the potentialities they have actualized, the meaning they have fulfilled, the values they have realized—and nothing and nobody can ever remove these assets from the past ... To be sure, people tend to see only the stubble fields of transitoriness but overlook and forget the full granaries of the past into which they have brought the harvest of their lives: the deeds done, the loves loved, and last but not least, the sufferings they have gone through with courage and dignity.[134]

It strikes me that the sooner we start to reflect on our lives, our achievements and the goals we still have, the more likely we will accept and take solace in these things as we become older and frailer. Let us start now to celebrate the richness of human life lived with purpose and meaning!

The Precise Moment of Choice

My heart knows what is important
When I slow down and listen
It kindly reminds me of the simple truth
Each small habit I have makes up the total of how I live
Not the job I do, the house where I live, who I love or what I say
But the choices I make each minute, that sculpt my life
A better life doesn't come from wishing or wanting
Complaining or resenting
Not from therapy or pushing or trying harder
But from the still moments between a
Thought and its action
The precise moment when I can choose
To notice those spaces
Between impulse and action
Between thought and deed
Is to choose consciously how I want to live
Not the habitual life I have settled for
Or the hurried life I have manufactured
Nor the fantasy life I have imagined
But the mindful life I choose in the precious moments
When I breathe out, before I breathe in
That knows what I really want

> *Without guilt or shame, shoulds or have tos*
> *Those precious moments that lead me back to my heart*
> *That knows what is indeed important*
> *And create for me the life I desire*
> *No blinding flash of enlightenment, but*
> *the soothing spread of contentment*
> *When my deepest inner needs and aspirations*
> *Are reflected in the living of each day*
>
> Jane O'Shea, *www.wordremedies.co.nz* [135]

Spirituality

To identify meaning and purpose we must first have a belief system through which we make sense of the world around us, and which gives that sense of connection to something greater than ourselves. This belief system we call spirituality. Living life with meaning and purpose is the foundation of a spiritual life. Spirituality means different things to different people; it can refer to everything from formal religion through to an umbrella term for a person's search for meaning and purpose in life. Traditionally, spirituality referred to a religious process, but now spirituality is seen to be more than simply religion. Kaplan and Berkman, in their book *Religion and Spirituality in Older People*, explain it this way:

> Religion is viewed as more institutionally based, more structured, and involving more traditional activities, rituals and practices. Spirituality refers to the intangible and immaterial and thus may be considered a more general term, not associated with a particular group or organization.[136]

How do you perceive spirituality? I have heard various descriptions in the group conversations I have led, such as: 'having a sense of a connection to something bigger than ourselves and it typically includes a search for our deepest values and meaning in life', 'it is more an individual practice and has to do with a sense of peace, purpose and love', 'a deep interconnection with ourselves, others and nature', and 'it relates to the process of developing beliefs around the meaning of life and your connection to others'.

It is interesting to note that the various descriptions include the words 'meaning', 'purpose' and 'others', individual, personal inner journeys and deeper self-reflections on what is important to help us gain an understanding of what gives life a deeper meaning. At this stage in life, you likely have come to realise that spirituality is a reflective lifelong journey.

You can practice spirituality in a religious manner and connect with a religion such as Islam, Buddhism, Christianity or Judaism. Or you may choose to practice a non-religious ideology and a more philosophical approach, such as atheism, agnosticism or humanism, or one of the many other practices around how people connect to the spiritual and transcendent. Or you may choose to subscribe to no spiritual ideology—religious or otherwise—and have your own inner beliefs. These days, it is not necessarily a given that you practice the religion you grew up with, or that you grew up with any religion at all. Spirituality, therefore, is not about your religious or non-religious affiliation; it is about whatever is meaningful and alive in you.

Here are some questions which help to explore what is important to you on a deeper and more spiritual level. Place your focus on the things that matter and make some notes in your journal.

- Do you have a sense of something greater in your life?
- If so, how do you experience that?
- How would you describe your authentic or 'true' self?
- What gives your life meaning and purpose?
- What values do you want to live by?
- Do your values guide your decisions and actions?

- How do you get through difficult times? Where do you find comfort?
- What makes your soul sing?

There is no point in asking: What is the meaning of life?; the question is better framed as What is the meaning of *my* life? Seeking purpose, meaning and understanding of what is sacred to us is intertwined in our day-to-day living, not always at the forefront of our thinking but subtly woven through our being. For many people there is a longing for meaning and search for an understanding of our existence, of who we are and what our gift is to life. We derive meaning and understanding of our life through the telling of our stories. This sharing ties together our past, present and future, integrating the multiple themes of who we are and where we have contributed to this world. Listening to or reading stories of other people's lives helps me to make sense of my world, of how I experience life, who I am and what matters to me. I wonder if this may also be your experience. Seeking and searching lead us to transformation, making changes to the way we live, whatever our age.

Activity: purposeful living

Reflection and journaling on living purposefully. What do I have to offer?
- What do older people in general offer a neighbourhood and community?
- What have you always wanted to contribute?
- What are you interested in or passionate about?
- What is your legacy?
- What defines you?
- What gives your life meaning?
- Do you think about your future and make plans?
- What do you look forward to now?

As a follow-up to this activity, consider a time when you felt centred, balanced: exactly who and where you wanted to be, living your life with meaning and purpose and feeling you were making a difference.

- Where was this?
- When was this and how long did this last?
- Who was there?
- What happened?
- How did you experience this at the time?
- How did you experience this over time?
- Is this experience reflected in some way in your present life?
- Describe what traces of this experience you see in your life now, if any.
- What is it that tells you that this experience is part of your core, your centre?

Find another person, a friend, a spouse or family member, and share your experiences to explore together what gives life meaning and what defines each of you. How do you see your transition into the second part or later stage of life? Listen to each other and then reflect upon your discussions—what did you hear, and what did you understand about each other's stories?

Activity: Write a letter to your future self

Here is another activity. You may choose to do this on your own with your journal, or with your conversation buddy. Describe yourself as you imagine you will be in ten years' time. What have you done in the past ten years that you enjoyed? What was important to you? Be specific. Now write a letter from your ten-year-older self to yourself at your current age. What would you tell yourself? What interest would you urge yourself to pursue? What dreams would you foster? What would you encourage yourself to put in place in preparation for your ageing future?[137]

Transformation

I offer you peace.
I offer you love.
I offer you friendship.
I see your beauty.
I hear your need.
I feel your feelings.
My wisdom flows from the Highest Source.
I greet that source in you.
Let us work together. For unity and love.

Mahatma Gandhi[138]

CHAPTER 9

Planning for End of Life

Do you feel a reluctance when reading the title of this conversation? If yes, you are not alone. Within Australia the uptake of advance care planning (the considered process of planning your current and future health care, incorporation your values, beliefs and preferences)[139] has been slow. When it happens, it is often initiated by a health professional at a time of crisis when you are in need of medical support. It appears that there is a reluctance to acknowledge impending mortality. Most individuals, and this includes health professionals,[140] find it difficult or uncomfortable to think and talk about death. However, we need to face reality; we are all going to die. I read a wonderful quote on celebrant Abby Buckley's website, which opens with the question: 'What is the current mortality rate in Australia? Answer: Despite huge advantages in modern medicine, the mortality rate continues to be 100%!'[141]

We are born, we live, and we die, although, due to advances in medicine and technology that save us from many diseases, we are generally living longer than previous generations. And, for some of us, this means we live with multiple and debilitating chronic diseases that will eventually lead to frailty and death. As with birth, dying is a process. How does it unfold, and can we prepare for it? We make plans and prepare for the birth of a child but somehow we give little thought to our end of life. Maybe we should consider some of the preparing for

a new life advice as equally relevant for preparing for a life soon to end. For example, comparing the two:
1. Be prepared: if you are anxious or afraid, inform yourself.
2. Reject negativity: don't engage in or listen to horror stories around dying. By planning you are likely to be much more in charge of the process.
3. Join a class or attend a workshop: have a conversation about death and what you can do to prepare.
4. Seek support and share your fears: you don't need to go it alone, seek emotional and physical support.
5. Set the scene: think about what would be the most comfortable environment to enable you to die peacefully, and consider if it is realistic.
6. Relax: be at ease with your imminent death—it is inevitable so make it the best you can—and know what helps you to be physically and emotionally comfortable.
7. Stay true to yourself: think honestly about what is important for you, and share this with your loved ones and medical team.

We are all going to die; yet in many western societies we do not consider, prepare for, or talk about death enough. Some people think it is morbid or depressing, but our planning and realistic thinking can enable us to meet death better prepared and more peacefully. What will it take to set aside our fears and discomfort around death and dying? Let's have an end of life conversation and think about making plans for our end of life support and care. To start these conversations, I can highly recommend Michael Hebb's book *Let's Talk About Death Over Dinner* where each chapter has a conversation prompt such as: 'Why don't we talk about death?' or 'What does a good death look like?'[142] Michael hosts dinner parties and the topic of discussion is, in one way or another, always about death. We seem to have a lot of anxiety about our last years, months and days and our ultimate death and tend to push away thoughts around mortality. However, it is healthier to have these conversations early and regularly. We may still be young and we may still be healthy, but we all have stories about people we knew who have died: our parents, our loved ones, our neighbours, our friends. Death does not always come after a long life; we can meet it at any age.

Consider becoming comfortable talking about being mortal. Take your time thinking about this topic, gain some clarity around your care wishes and consider what is important to you.

As I mentioned earlier, most of my clients and conversation participants expressed their wish to live and die at home. A report by the Grattan Institute confirms this, stating:

> People want to die comfortable at home, supported by family and friends and effective services. But dying in Australia is more institutionalised than in the rest of the world ... Surveys consistently show that between 60 and 70 per cent of Australians would prefer to die at home. [Yet] only about 14 per cent of people die at home.[143]

Professor Ken Hillman, Professor of Intensive Care at the University of NSW, believes we are doing it all wrong and asks why so many elderly people linger in pain and confusion in intensive care units when all they want to do is die in peace at home with their loved ones. I attended a most inspirational presentation by Professor Hillman in March 2018 titled 'Care consideration for the frail elderly at the end of life'. That presentation deeply moved me and has encouraged me to have open and honest conversations with people, and not only with frail older people, by asking them what their wishes are for their end of life. I highly recommend before you read further you watch Hillman's TEDxSydney talk: 'We're doing dying all wrong'.[144] It's less than 15 minutes long. If you don't have access to a computer and the internet at home, your local library will most likely be able to help you access the video. Hillman said: 'This is one of the most important decisions in your life. You need to take control over your own end of life.'

What do you think? Did you find this TED talk thought provoking? What thoughts, feelings or emotions came up for you? Will this presentation inspire you to determine your values, your goals and your preferences for your end of life? Dr. Atul Gawande, a surgeon, public health researcher and author, fully agrees with Hillman. In his book *Being Mortal* Gawande writes:

> as people's capacity wane, whether through age or ill health, making their lives better often requires curbing our purely medical imperatives—resisting the urge to fiddle and fix and control. It was not hard to see how important this idea could be for the patients I encountered in my daily practice—people facing mortal circumstances at every phase of life. But it posed a difficult question: When should we try to fix and when should we not?[145]

Gawande goes on:

> People with serious illness have priorities besides simply prolonging their lives. Surveys find that their top concerns include avoiding suffering, strengthening relationships with family and friends, being mentally aware, not being a burden on others, and achieving a sense that their life is complete.[146]

One important way we can avoid some of the dilemmas around medical intervention at the end of life is to have the difficult conversations while we have the capacity, and write down and formalise an advance care plan.

Advance care plan and advance care directive

An advance care plan is a written plan which outlines your preferences, wishes and decisions around your future health care, while an advance care directive, according to the Australian Government Department of Health,[147] is a formalised and signed version of your end of life advance care plan.

An advance care plan will be different for each person and varies depending on health, wealth, age and cultural factors. It is important that everyone, regardless of age and current health, considers their future care needs and make their wishes clear to their family, loved ones and medical practitioners. These plans are not only important for older people: anyone can experience a catastrophic injury or illness, and should consider recording their wishes in case, for instance, they suffer a brain injury or severe paralysis.

Check out Advance Care Planning Australia website as it provides valuable up-to-date information, free expert advice, and stories and video clips of the lived experiences in advance care planning of individuals, families and carers. It is a national program funded by the Australian Government Department of Health, designed to help Australians make the best choices for their future health and care.[148] When I facilitate a conversation series and we reach this topic, I show the group Hillman's TED talk and the video clip from Advance Care Planning Australia, 'Advance Care Planning 1: Starting the conversation'. You can also find this on YouTube.[149]

After watching these video clips, we start the conversation with open questions:
- What resonates?
- What are you curious about?
- What matters to you most?
- What concerns do you have?
- What personal experiences influence your thinking?
- Who do you want to have an end of life conversation with?
- Have you prepared an advance care plan?

In a non-threatening environment with others their age, people will start talking and share stories of experiences around death and dying and care provision. There are beautiful and supportive care stories around end of life and there are the horror stories we all hope will not happen to us. In a group of 12 to 15, there are people who have an advance care plan in place, some who are considering their advance care plans, and there will inevitably be several people in each group who have not made any future end of life plans. This conversation topic gets people talking. What inspires me is that participants are supportive of each other and willing to share their experiences and offer help and support. What I have witnessed is that some participants decide as a group to continue to meet and further these conversations in an informal way. The conversation group gets the ball rolling, so to speak, and it motivates individuals to deeply think about their end of life wishes.

Preparing an advance care plan enables you to make and document your choices for your end of life care while you are still well and able to make informed choices. Having taken the time to consider your needs, also make time to discuss your wishes with your family and loved ones before completing and signing an official advance care directive. This document gives you peace of mind and ensures, as much as is possible, that you continue to have a quality of life of *your* choice until the end. Talking about and preparing an advance care directive helps you to keep or take control over your own end of life, and having documentation in place helps your family and loved ones in conveying your wishes to the care providers if you are no longer able to do so yourself. For the loved ones left behind, an advance care directive removes the burden for them of wondering, while they may be dealing with a crisis, what your wishes might be. A fully signed-off advance care directive will contain all your needs and preferences for your future care, along with your beliefs, values and goals.

My friend Merily was reluctant to talk about the frail-aged stage of life. As she said: 'the cancer will kill me before I get old', but because she knew my work and interest in supporting people to age and die well, we did engage in discussions on ageing, death and dying. Slowly but surely she considered what was important to her and that, however she died—from cancer or a natural death through advanced age—Merily came to a realisation that advance care planning was relevant to her too. After some months, during one of our walks together, Merily said, 'Lia, you will be proud of me, as I have considered my future care plans and did complete my advance care directive. I have discussed my wishes with my partner, children, GP and specialist, and they each have a copy of my directions.' Merily was right: she did not get to the frail-aged stage of life, her cancer killed her within six years of her diagnosis. But her family knew and respected her wishes and that supported Merily to live and die on her own terms.

When completing an advance care directive, as well as listing your preferences for your care at your end of life, you will also need to appoint a substitute decision maker for if or when the time comes that you are no longer able to make decisions yourself. This person could be a partner, friend or family member. It is probably easier if the person is available, readily contactable and lives in the same city or region and therefore able to be present in person should the need arise.

Power of attorney (POA)

In addition to recording your end of life wishes, there may come a time when you will need support to manage your medical, financial or personal affairs. Who will help you make the decisions? When you sign an advance care directive you can also formally appoint a substitute decision maker for a time when you may no longer be able to make decisions for yourself. Each Australian State and Territory has its own laws governing guardianship and powers of attorney so please check the relevant guidelines and check the My Aged Care website for up-to-date legal information. So do your homework, check your local regulations, if you need to you can consult a lawyer who specialises in elder law, and appoint your decision maker POA. An enduring power of attorney (EPOA) is a decision maker you have legally appointed who will make financial and legal decisions on your behalf *after you lose capacity* to make your own decisions. A medical power of attorney is a decision maker you have appointed who will have the authority to make medical decision on your behalf. They can be, but need not be, the same person.

Making a will

Even if you have already made a will, it is a good idea to check and update it from time to time. Circumstances change, or we may change our minds as we age and find different priorities. Many of us have heard terrible, sad stories about people dying without a well-thought-through will. For example: Harry and Mary have three adult children but no will. Mary dies leaving the full estate to Harry, not to the children. Harry meets Trudy who has two adult children, and remarries. Still Harry has not made a will. Harry has a heart attack and dies, and therefore the estate goes to Trudy. Trudy lives a bit longer but eventually she dies and now, as there is no will in place, all the estate goes to her two children and none to Mary and Harry's children. This is a rather simplistic version, but it happens, and it happens a lot. And yes, Mary and Harry's three children can take legal action, but the big winners are the legal firms. Avoid all this stress and expense by having a will that has been reviewed by a legal professional to ensure it is legitimate; that way, you can be sure that your estate is distributed according to your wishes and you thereby reduce the risk of your will being contested. If you do not make decisions about the division of your estate by making a valid will, the law of whichever state or territory you lived in will determine how your estate is divided.

Organ or tissue donation

Another end of life decision that is important to consider is organ and tissue donation. Australia has a low rate of organ donation compared to many other countries and, sadly, even when a person had decided to be a donor, family members can override the decisions. Organ and tissue donations can not only transform people's lives but save them. While some people have religious objections to donation, it is worth careful consideration by most of us, even if we may feel uncomfortable about it.

You can donate an organ while you are alive but generally donation takes place after your death. The organs used are heart, kidneys, liver, lungs, pancreas, and large intestine, and the body tissues used are heart tissue or valves, blood veins, skin, bone, ligaments and tendons, part of the eye, pancreas tissues and amniotic tissue. The Australian Government Organ and Tissues Authority website offers a lot of resources that can help you think about donation and in your conversations with family and friends. If you would like to register as an organ or tissue donor, go to the website[150] or ring (02) 5156 6662. Some of you may already have registered as an organ donor, and it is important to have conversations with family so that they understand your wish to donate and respect your wishes at the time of your death.

Organise and dispose of your 'stuff'

Planning and completing the documentation of your advance care directive, the power of attorney and your will are the practical and, in a way, must-do preparations for your end of life planning. But have you considered the emotional side of dying? Have you thought of what you could do or plan that gives your death more meaning and makes it less difficult for you and your loved ones? I am a practical person and believe in sorting out my 'stuff'. My 'stuff' is likely of little interest or value to others in my family. I do like a bit of annual spring cleaning to sort out the attic, my office and cupboards to work out what I still want or need to keep, what I would like to give away to friends and family, what I can send to the 'op' shop, or what needs to go in the bin. I do not believe I need to burden my family with all my 'stuff' when I am gone. It is an act of kindness to those you love.

I am also giving thought to some of my 'special things' and consider who would like to have these on my death. Here I think of my jewellery, some artwork and other little trinkets. These may not be of high financial value, but they are of emotional and spiritual value to me. Some years ago, my mother-in-law, while we were all together for a family wedding, invited each of her grandchildren in turn to her 'special cabinet' to choose something they would like to remember her by. One of my daughters has Nana's coffee cup and small footstool, which reminds her of her Nana and the place she had in her life. These keepsakes, large and small, spark conversations as often there is a memory or story attached.

An emotional will

Before you die you may like to write an emotional will. The Groundswell Project states that

> An emotional will is about your legacy. It is a way to share your thoughts, values, lessons in life, passions, hopes and dreams with your family, friends, and future generations. This is your chance to ensure that you don't leave this life with things left unsaid.[151]

Their website has a brochure you can download titled, 'Your emotional will', which may help you communicate your wishes to your loved ones. Note that it is *not* a legal document. In chapter seven, I mentioned Australian palliative care nurse Bronnie Ware who documented her patient's thoughts and regrets over the last weeks of their lives. What would you still like to complete or talk about with others? Are there important relationships to mend? Disagreements and old wounds to heal before it is too late? Have those difficult conversations and make sure you say what you want to say. Give or ask for forgiveness, make amends. Thank people and tell them you love them. Gratitude and love are what is most needed at the end of life. If you find it too difficult to say these words in person, write a letter. You can give or send this letter before you die or leave it with your other legal documents.

Leaving a legacy can be about telling the story of your life. Leave behind the story of your experiences, the people you met and who made an impression, funny incidents, special moments, the ideas or work that mattered to you. If you have such stories, add them to your children's and the family history. If not your family, then give them to good and dear friends. Our lives and our contributions matter, all of us play an important role in what we call human life.

Keep your emotional will in a folder with all the other legal documents related to your end of life planning. This folder should also contain details of any health or life insurance, your bank and superannuation accounts and any subscriptions, as well as your will; funeral plans; contact details of people you would like to be informed of your death; passwords for computer, emails, social media networks, etc.; and the letters you may have written. Keep them safe and let your appointed person(s) know where they can find them. If you live in a bushfire-prone area of the country, remember to put them in your bushfire preparation box. Better still, make a few copies and give them to a careful friend or family member.

Place of death

With all the legal documentation related to living, dying and a will out of the way, let's have a conversation about how and where you would like to die, if you were to have a choice. As I have written, most people have a preference to die at home as that is where they feel safe and most comfortable, and their last weeks and days of life can continue as 'normal'. However, there can be good reason to spend the last part of your life in a hospital, hospice or nursing home. You may not feel safe or cared for at home, you may be living on your own and there is no or only limited carer support available, or you may have a medical condition that requires you to be cared for in hospital or nursing home. Each option has positive and negative aspects. Let's talk about some of the places you could choose.

Dying in a hospital

This allows you to have full medical and nursing care present, and your family can be with you for as long as they wish (assuming there are no infectious disease pandemics prevalent at the time!). A hospital is likely to have a single room for the dying person, which allows for some privacy. However, a hospital is a very hectic place and staff will often be in and out, sometimes leaving little time for being together quietly with your loved ones. A hospital will have rules and guidelines about what and when activities such as meals, sleeping, visitors, and nursing and doctors' rounds are possible. A hospital is geared towards medical intervention and short-term stays, and therefore different to a hospice.

Dying in a hospice

A hospice is a place which specialises in the care of people who are in their terminal stage of life. It is smaller than a hospital and more 'home like'. You will have your own room and bathroom and you can bring some of your small treasures from home. Visitors can come and go more freely, pending health restrictions, and there are fewer rules around eating, drinking and sleeping. Care will be provided by a specialist palliative care team, carers and volunteers.

Merily had a strong preference for dying in a hospice as she did not want to be a burden on her family or friends. In particular, she did not want to be a burden on her daughter who has a young family. Merily wanted to be in a hospice where she would be cared for by professional staff and with her immediate family by her side. Sadly, she was in the hospice during the Covid-19 pandemic in 2020, so there were restrictions on the number of visitors she could receive, but it was still an environment that, for Merily, was preferable to being at home or in hospital.

A year after Merily's death in hospice care, her daughter Frida shared an experience of her mother's days at the hospice, where she received good quality palliative care.

> I think the hardest part was that no-one in the hospice really knew her story, or knew her. I was trying to get her home but it turned out she was too sick for that transition to happen. And although the nurses provided care for her, and were caring, they didn't actually

care. It didn't make any difference to them if she were there or not. Not really. That mattered to me, I am not sure why. I put up photos on the wall of Mum—Mum as Mum was before she got ill. To give some sense of who she was. Because that person that was left in the bed at the end was so unlike Mum in real life. My real Mum.

Dying in residential aged care/nursing home

For people who have been living in residential care, this would be like dying 'at home' for them. Their GP will take responsibility for medical care needs and routine care and nursing will be provided by the staff in the home. Often a resident can die in their own room, or they may have to be transferred to a more specialised sick bay within the home. If the care required is too intensive or needs technical equipment, transfer to a hospital or hospice may be considered.

Dying at home

This enables you in to say goodbye to all who are dear to you and spend your last days in your own familiar and intimate environment with people you know and love. If it is your wish to be surrounded by your loved ones in a familiar environment then dying at home, with the support of a community palliative care team, may be something you wish to consider as an option.

What you *do* need to do is talk with your family about your wish to die at home. How would they feel about you dying in the bed and in the home that you shared together? Talk it over and discover how each family member feels about supporting dying at home, and what each member considers as the positives as well as the challenges. What is also important to consider when choosing to die at home is what daily support will be available to help with all the care and practical organisational requirements. This is to ensure that your family and friends directly engaged in supporting you as you are dying are not overburdened, and do not become stressed or burn out. To die at home, you need the support of people who are willing and can make the time to be there for you. Most often family wish to be there to support the dying person. You might also consider others, friends or neighbours, who are willing to be with the dying person to give the main care provider some time out. These extra support people could also provide some practical support with things like meal preparation, shopping and house cleaning. Choose the support you would like to have around you and, most importantly, ask if people are comfortable helping. On the whole people are willing to help but they often feel that they would not like to intrude.

Palliative care

Palliative care is for people who have a serious and life-limited illness, one which cannot be cured such as cancer or end of life organ diseases like those of the heart, lungs or liver. It provides the care and support people require in their last phase of life. The goal of palliative care is for you to experience this period as comfortable as is possible and to enable you to do what is still important to you. A palliative care team of compassionate specialists establish, in conversation with you and in consultation with your doctor, what your needs are and how and with whom you wish to spend your final days. Palliative care manages symptoms such as pain, discomfort, tiredness and dehydration and aims to improve the quality of your life at its end. Your palliative care team will be able to discuss with you and help you make a choice about staying at home or moving to a hospice when the time comes. The team will be able to advise you where to get psychological, emotional or spiritual support; they can make suggestions about support groups, such as those for various cancers or diseases, where you are able to meet people with similar lived experiences. Contact your local state palliative care team or Palliative Care Australia, the umbrella organisation,[152] and become familiar with all that palliative care can offer in the last phase of your life.

Death or end of life doulas

Along with your palliative care team, you could engage the support of a death (or end of life) doula. This is a trained, *non-medical* person who provides emotional, social, spiritual, educational and practical support aligned with their client's wishes. A death doula can support the dying person and family through death and beyond. There is no governing body for end of life doulas in Australia, nor Federal or state government accreditation, so be sure to make yourself well-informed before engaging a doula. There is a Sydney-based doula college you could contact for further details.[153]

Gather information that is relevant to you, discuss it with your health professional and gain an understanding of what it means. The more we engage in these conversations to understand about death, the better prepared we are. It helps us to understand the process and to reconcile with it, which in turn can lead to a more peaceful death.

Euthanasia: voluntary assisted dying

This can be a contentious topic around which people can have religious, ethical and moral viewpoints. However, it is a choice which some are keen to explore. Euthanasia, or voluntary assisted dying, is the intentional ending of life to relieve suffering for those who are at the end of life. 'Voluntary assisted dying (euthanasia and assisted dying) (VAD) is a major legal, ethical and social policy issue with significant implications for health systems, health professionals and communities around the world', according to the Australian Centre for Health Law Research.[154] Each country has its own laws around euthanasia and assisted dying. In Australia, the law governing voluntary assisted dying is state or territory based; you must therefore check the regulations in your local jurisdiction.

I would like to tell you about my goddaughter Lucy, who lived in the Netherlands. In 2020, Lucy, the second daughter of my eldest brother, died an assisted death at age 50, having lived with cancer for twenty years. She did not 'battle' or 'fight' with cancer; no, she lived with cancer. This was not easy for her or her loving husband and two young daughters. Together they lived life, with all its ups and downs, to the fullest. Lucy was supported by a good medical team and by all medical treatment available for her. However, every few years her medical condition changed and her health and wellbeing deteriorated, which meant that further adjustments to life needed to be made. Lucy and her family did this with great courage. Six weeks before she died, Lucy suffered numerous brain infarcts (strokes) and her medical team told her, after a successful surgery to remove a brain clot, that there was nothing more they could do for her. With support from her family and friends, Lucy went home. She realised that time was running out as it became increasingly more difficult to live with the pain and with all the support and intervention she now needed in all her daily activities. In those last few weeks Lucy and her family made the decision to choose an assisted death. It was time to say goodbye. This decision provided Lucy with the opportunity to fully plan for her exit from life, and her funeral, and she did this fearlessly, knowing that she had the full support of her family by her side at home. What I admire in Lucy was that she was always able to talk openly about living with cancer and her likely early death.

Lucy and her family lived with death for many years. It was difficult, painful, life restricting, anxiety provoking, deeply sad and yet, strangely, there was also a deep and meaningful richness to their lives. Lucy and her family always openly discussed the challenges and options they faced, and together they made their choices, they had the difficult conversations. I cannot stress the importance, particularly as you grow older, of having these conversations while you are still in good health and have the time and cognitive ability to consider options and plan. Talking with your family and your GP about mortality enables you to consider your options, make informed decisions and instigate plans for your future. Waiting until a stressful time, such as during a hospital admission or needing to enter residential care, will more than likely not give you the outcomes you are hoping for. Get your end of life affairs in order so you can get on with living your life!

Where to from here?

Ok, so you've read and thought about all that we've discussed in this chapter so far. You've done the thinking, now it's time for the doing! So:
- document your wishes in your advance care directive
- identify your decision maker
- arrange your enduring power of attorney
- make a will or review your will
- consider organ and tissue donation
- consider preparing an emotional will
- consider and document your funeral and burial planning wishes.

We will have a conversation about funeral and burial planning in the next chapter.

I leave you with a few questions to ponder.

Activity

Activities around your end of life and death may make your shudder but fear not! We know we are all going to die, and don't you want to ensure that your end of life and death are to *your* wishes, and not someone else's—indeed, possibly even the decisions of a complete stranger? Have your journal ready to record your thoughts.

So, start with asking yourself a few basic questions:
- Do you talk about death, with family, friends or other acquaintances?
- If not, why not?
- Would you like to talk about death?
- What is stopping you from talking about death?

Moving on to the practicalities:
- Do you have an advance care directive, will and power of attorney in place? If not, why not? And if yes, are they up to date?

- Organ donation, would you want to consider this? If so, register as a donor and inform your family of your decision.

Now some potentially uncomfortable questions:
- Who would you have a conversation with?
- What are the important things you want to talk about?
- What would a 'good' death look like to you?
- If you had only 30 days left to live, how would you spend them? Your last day? Your last hour?
- Have you been part of an end of life experience?
- How do you want to feel in your final days and hours?
- Where do you want to be when you die?

Artistic activity: fears and challenges, opportunities and courage

For this activity use quality paper, soft or oil pastels and/or colouring in pencils.

1. Consider what comes to mind when you think of the fears and challenges of end of life. Draw images, use colours, words or phrases that help you express and connect to this.
2. Take another sheet of paper and write what you want or would like at the end of your life. Does it align with your end of life wishes as recorded in your advance care directive? What are the opportunities for a different experience? What or who could you draw upon to help you realise your wishes? How do you overcome the fears and challenges identified in the first picture? Imagine the opportunities and courage, and use images, colours, words, or phrases that connect to how you feel yourself overcoming the obstacles and fears.
3. This is the integration component: take a third piece of paper and evolve an image from the significant parts of the fears and challenges picture, but then add aspects of the opportunities and courage picture in ways that change and transform the overall

image. Through this process of integrating the two images the nature of the fears and challenges we face can be altered in acknowledging ways that the experience can be different.

Resources

Websites

The Groundswell Project: an Australian-based organisation that assists people in end of life planning. Its website states: 'we must socialise the conversation about death, dying and bereavement by providing opportunities for the community to re-develop a shared language for talking and planning for end of life using local resources and information. This helps to build people's death literacy and connects people to one another, where they live and online.' Its website has a huge range of information and links to other useful organisations: www.thegroundswellproject.com. You can contact Groundswell by email or mail: info@thegroundswellproject.com or The GroundSwell Project, PO Box 626, Marrickville NSW 1425

Palliative Care Australia: for information on end of life care: www.palliativecare.org.au or email: pca@palliativecare.org.au; or ring head office, 02 6232 0700; NSW 02 8076 5600; SA, 08 8271 1643; Qld, 07 3842 3242; Vic, 03 9662 9644; WA, 1300 551 704; Tas, 03 6231 2799; ACT, 02 6255 5771; NT, 08 8951 6762

'The inappropriate question', 2020, a video by Professor Joseph Ibrahim (https://www.profjoe.com.au/), on the pros and cons of cardiopulmonary resuscitation (CPR), especially as we age, https://www.youtube.com/watch?v=30eXWq80E00

My Values: https://www.myvalues.org.au This website has a very good questionnaire, compiles a report on your responses and allows you to share the report with others such as family and GP. You can also amend the report whenever you like.

Recommended reading

K. Hillman. 2017. *A Good Life to the End: Taking control of our inevitable journey through ageing and death.* Allen & Unwin, Crows Nest, NSW.

A. Gawande. 2015. *Being Mortal: Illness, medicine, and what matters in the end.* Profile Books, London.

CHAPTER 10

Planning for Your Funeral

'What do you mean, planning for my funeral? Why would I? I will be dead and not there to worry about it!' Not everyone likes to consider their future death and even less consider what their funeral will be like. It is not something people enjoy talking about, and quite simply, it is not a hot topic of conversation. We speak about most things related to death, dying or funerals, for that matter, in hushed voices instead of making it a robust and stimulating discussion. I believe the reason to plan for your funeral is quite simple. If you do not provide some guidelines or make some plans for your funeral, your family will have to make those arrangements at a time of grief and distress. Furthermore, most of us have been able to make choices about how we live our lives, why shouldn't we want to make sure that the final chapter is also what we wish?

Funerals can be difficult and also be extremely stressful for those left behind. There can be fraught family discussion around how much to spend or whether the deceased really did want a cremation. If you consider what you want, discuss it with your family, make plans and provide some guidelines, much of this stress will be alleviated, and you can ensure you have the funeral that you want. Do you want a big and elaborate funeral that can be attended by all your friends and family? Do you want a church service or a civil ceremony, to be buried or cremated?

Where do you want to be buried or have your ashes held? Do you want a headstone and if you do, what do you want written on it? Do you want people to worry far less about the formalities of a conventional funeral and simply have a great party to celebrate your life?

The financial aspect does, sadly, also need to be considered. I am not suggesting you pre-pay for a funeral plan as that may not be the most cost effective choice, but it may be helpful to set some funds aside for when the time comes. Leave your affairs in order; the following are some questions from an article by Kate Browne, 'What to do when someone dies' that may be helpful, whether you are arranging your own funeral or someone else's:

> Are there any sickness, accident, life, superannuation or private health insurance policies that could pay towards the funeral? Was the deceased a returned service person or did they belong to any club, pensioner association or trade union that may entitle them to a payment to help cover funeral costs? If you or the deceased person received payments from Centrelink, check with Centrelink about a possible bereavement payment or allowance.[155]

Forward planning usually saves money and provides you with well-considered and better options, and the outcome you want. It also relieves those left behind of unexpected expense.

Consider this scenario: you would like to be buried but your loved ones are not aware of this as they assume you have always had a wish to be cremated. Here is my personal story. My will and future directions had not been updated for numerous years and my previously expressed wishes were indeed for my body to be cremated. As I am becoming more aware of the environmental footprint of my life, I have since changed my thinking and explored more environmentally friendly options for disposing of my body. This I have now documented and discussed with my husband and children. Our adult children are in the midst of living their life and raising their children and are not ready, nor have the time, to consider death and funerals but they were willing to engage in conversation, a great topic over (Christmas) lunch! We had some fun, made plenty of 'death' jokes, explored options and considered seriously what could be a suitable funeral. With their support I was able to insert their valuable suggestions in my funeral plan and acknowledged that this, for them, is also part of their celebration of my life.

Planning for your funeral has many advantages and it is a lot easier when 'the end' is not near. By sharing your wishes with your family, you ensure that you will have a funeral which is most suited to your lifestyle and choices. It eases the confusion, guess work and decision-making processes for your relatives—which is important in a time of grief. Planning your funeral according to your wishes provides you with an opportunity to check out viability and an overview of costing. Knowing an approximate cost will enable you to set some funds aside. A positive and well-planned funeral has healing qualities for the grieving process. It is one last and comforting memory of you.

Lucy, my niece, talked about her cancer and her likely early death and she made her preparations. I believe Lucy had been preparing for a while and in particular with her immediate family, her husband and two teenage daughters. She lovingly and openly shared and talked about living and how dying is part of life. In her final weeks Lucy said her goodbyes, shared her love and gifts to all who were dear to her and she planned her funeral with her family. In her eulogy, her mother spoke about how they laughed and shared the poetry Lucy had written over the years and how they chose the ones to be read during the service. Lucy's love and emotional support was there in spirit for each of us. In all the words offered at the funeral, Lucy's love shone through. What I learned from Lucy over the years of her illness were her messages on life: the importance of love, connections with others and mutual support, her enjoyment of nature in all its beauty, and living of life in all honesty with all that is offered.

You may have previously engaged in funeral planning for a parent, relative or friend, and you will know that there are a lot of matters you need to consider. At the time, you may have had thoughts about what you would like or do differently if it was your funeral. Here is your opportunity!

What to consider when planning for your funeral

Online you will find numerous funeral planning checklists and each of them provide prompts or questions for you to contemplate. As you start to explore them you will see that there really are many options. It is the duty of your executor to arrange your funeral so give them a copy of or link to this information. And remember that including your funeral wishes in your will is not enough: in most cases the will is not read until after the funeral.[156]

The National Death Advocacy Network (NDAN) is a growing Australian network and advocacy partnership of community facilitators, professionals, activists, and educators working to enrich the experience of dying and death, and they could provide some helpful initial hints and support in working out and preparing for your funeral.[157] Another useful website is Gathered Here, which has a large Australian database of funeral service providers. You will find information on comparing funeral services and funeral pricing, and it provides a guide to environmentally friendly funeral options in Australia.[158] Further, I recommend you read the article by *Choice*: 'Lifting the lid on funerals',[159] which examines your funeral options and the impact on your pocket and the planet. The list of prompts you find in this chapter is compiled from a variety of sources. The links to some of these sites you will find at the end of this chapter.

Who to notify when death occurs

If a person dies in a hospital, hospice or residential facility, the staff will arrange for a doctor to issue a notification and Doctor's Certificate of Cause of Death and notify the authorities.

If a person dies at home, you or your funeral director will need to contact the person's GP or regular doctor, who will issue a Doctor's Certificate of Cause of Death—unless the death at home was unexpected, in which case you would need to ring the police. It will then depend on the circumstances if a coroner is required to conduct a post-mortem to determine the cause of death.

Be aware that the Doctor's Certificate of Cause of Death is not the same document as an official death certificate, which is issued by the Registry of Births, Deaths and Marriages in your state. A death must be registered, usually within one month of death. This is usually part of a funeral package; if not, the executor will need to do it.[160]

Notify family and friends as soon as is practical so they hear the sad news in the kindest way possible, and from loved ones rather than the 'grapevine' or a newspaper obituary. For this, as part of your funeral planning, prepare a list of names and contact phone numbers. Contact immediate family and loved ones first in case they would like to have a special time with the deceased person on their own or as part of a family or inner circle. Allow yourselves this special and precious time.

Organ donation

We had a conversation earlier around the option of organ donation during the discussion of our end of life planning topic. As an organ donor your organ(s) or body tissue could be used for organ and/or tissue transplant and you can also donate your body or organs to science research. To ascertain if there is a need for donating body parts to science you may have to check this out with universities as part of your planning. Kate Browne, in her article 'What to do when someone dies', advises: 'If you know the deceased had wished to donate their organs, it's important to move quickly because the process of donation needs to happen soon after death.'[161] So make sure, especially if you plan to die at home, that those around you know of your wishes and are appropriately prepared.

Choosing to go to a funeral home or to stay at home

If you die in a hospital, hospice or residential care facility you can choose to be taken to a funeral home or to your own home or the home of a relative or friend. It is not a requirement that you be taken to a funeral home; you have a choice. What would be your preference and what is possible for you? Do you want people to be able to be with you, or is that not your preference?

In a funeral home your body will be placed in the mortuary and a viewing is possible on arrangement for family and friends in a private and quiet viewing room.

Keeping the body at home saves money and is possible, even if the person has died in hospital, but it needs to be something that you would want, and you need to have the space in the house and make some necessary preparations for this to happen. Keeping the body of your loved one at home enables you to spend time with their body whenever you like, which can be an important part of the grieving process. See further below for considerations about keeping a body at home.

First, I will tell you a story about my first memory of death. It was when I was five years old and my 'Opa' had died. We visited Aunty Jane where the body of my grandfather was resting for five days before his funeral. In his final years of life, Opa had been living in turn with several of his children including with Aunty Jane. Also, Aunty Jane had a separate front room most suited for a coffin and private viewing. I stood at Opa's wooden coffin, which was open but covered with a glass plate, and just looked at his kind face. The coffin was lined with creamy coloured silk, and Opa was dressed in a light blue satin gown and he had his rosary beads in his folded hands—all in keeping with cultural and religious traditions of the day. Having the body at home, paying your respects to family, viewing the body, and saying goodbye to the deceased person was the norm for young and old in Dutch culture. It may not be the norm for your cultural background, but by planning your funeral you decide what it is that you want.

Funeral arrangements

In Australia there is no legal requirement to engage the services of a funeral director except, according to Kate Browne from *Choice*, 'In WA, you must use a licensed funeral director or obtain a permit from a cemetery board to arrange a funeral without one.' Otherwise, you and your relatives could make all the arrangements yourselves. The choice is yours; fully use the services and venue of a funeral home and director, use your own home, or have a family-organised and guided funeral, or consider a combination of the two. Work out your personal wishes based on your values and beliefs, discuss these with your relatives and friends and go about investigating how this is achievable.

A funeral home will provide advice and help you organise the whole event. A funeral director knows the process of making all the arrangements, which includes all the legal requirements. A funeral director can advise you on coffins or casket, body care, flowers, death notices, the funeral venue and more, as well as organise and book the crematorium or burial plot. If your choice is to let a funeral director make all the arrangements, shop around, and speak to several funeral providers (as well as your family and friends who may have been through the process) and request full pricing information to ensure you understand what services you are paying for and that you are paying a fair and reasonable price for the services provided. A funeral director will have the expertise and will be able to arrange a funeral service with no burden (apart from the financial) on you or your family.

In a family-led funeral, you and your family can be fully in control and take the responsibility of the funeral proceedings on as much or as little as you want and are able to. A family-led funeral is 'a term used to describe a funeral practice where the person who has died is cared for by the family and community from the moment of death, through to the delivery of the funeral ceremony, and up to the disposal of the body'.[162] This includes all official documentation, caring for the body, and organising rituals, gatherings and a funeral ceremony. If support or advice is needed, arrangements can be made with a funeral director as mentioned above, with an end of life doula or an independent funeral celebrant. Ensure that, if you seek outside support in the organisation or the implementation of the funeral plan, everyone is clear on the plan of action and the costs involved.

In home-based death care it is family and friends who provide care to the deceased person instead of funeral directors. Again, you could provide this care with as much or little support from professional funeral workers as you want. It is important to ensure that, within four to eight hours after the person has died, the body is kept cool at 5 degrees Celsius. You can achieve this by using a cool plate, a cooling blanket or ice pack, and air conditioners to keep the room cool.

In the case of home-based deaths, you will also need to provide respectful care of the body. The following procedures of care for the body are to be considered ahead of time in the decision-making process and for you to work out if this is welcomed and feasible within your family and friends' circle.

It is best to close the eyes of the deceased immediately after the person has died, a little Vaseline under the eyelids will help in keeping them closed. Also, if dentures have been removed over the last few days or hours, place these back into the mouth. To ensure the mouth remains closed, place a rolled-up cloth or towel under the chin or tie a cloth or tea-towel which has been placed under the chin on top to the head. This ensures the mouth remains closed while the body stiffens. The head tie can be removed when rigor mortis has set in. The chin roll can remain in place if needed.

It is suggested that the body is minimally washed to ensure the little layer of skin-oil remains in place as this helps the body to remain presentable for longer. If cleaning of some body parts is required use a little warm water and essential oils. Dress the deceased in pull-up incontinence pants as this is highly effective as a preventive to any leakage. When dressing the deceased consider clothing of natural fibres that are more environmentally friendly in decomposing and exclude nylon pantyhose and shoes. Then place the body on a cool plate in a coffin or wrap the body in a shroud and ensure the room is air-conditioned.

Coffin or casket

What is the difference? Coffins are narrower at the head and the feet and broader at the shoulders while a casket is rectangular in shape; both are traditionally made from timber. Caskets are used in most funerals in Australia. There are a variety on the market and they vary in price. And there is the option to make and decorate the coffin/casket yourself or with your relatives and friends.

Green burials

Within Australia there is a growing interest in natural burial. A 'green' or natural burial has the emphasis placed on simplicity and being environmentally friendly. The body is neither cremated nor prepared with chemicals such as embalming fluids; it is placed in a coffin or casket that is made of natural or recycled biodegradable materials, which is friendlier to our environment. The body in a coffin or shroud is interred in a grave and allowed to return to nature. Coffins can be made of natural fibres such as cardboard, wicker, grasses and bamboo. The internet has a wealth of information on how to make and decorate a coffin, making shrouds, where to buy shrouds, and so forth.

When I shared with my youngest daughter that I was writing the draft version of this chapter she sent me a link to a post about an eco-friendly 'living' coffin made from mushrooms, which has been designed by a Dutch bio designer. I was impressed and highly inspired! The coffin is made from mushroom fibre, mycelium, which apparently is a recycler and turns toxins into nutrients. Inside the coffin you see a bed of moss which ensures a lot of micro-organisms to help with the decomposition process. Apparently, once the coffin is buried you can water it, add seeds, and grow a tree. How is that for a natural burial! I used the words 'loop mushroom casket' in my search engine and indeed there were numerous articles and news items on the mushroom coffin.

A shroud

In simple terms, a shroud is a piece of fabric, preferably made from natural fibres, in which you wrap the body of a deceased person. The body can then be placed in a coffin or be cremated. According to Gathered Here's website on burial and cremation shrouds, it appears that in most states in Australia you are not permitted to use a burial shroud without a coffin, with the exception of Muslims or for burial at a natural burial site. Generally, most crematoriums do not allow the delivery of a body in a shroud as it makes handling the body more difficult; their preference is for a container with a solid base such as a timber body tray. If you want to be buried in a shroud, check this information with a funeral home, cemetery or crematorium in your area.

My personal thinking and preferences have been for a natural burial, being wrapped in a shroud. Several years ago, I saw some images of creatively designed and beautifully made wool felted shrouds and this encouraged me to consider making my own shroud. One day a friend invited me to go with her to a fabric shop neither of us had been to before, an opportunity to explore something new. While we were browsing we ran into an acquaintance, so we had a brief exchange. I had no sewing project in mind but after some time looking at the various fabrics, I found at the back of the store the wool fabric section, where I saw a wonderful bolt of warm red wool fabric. 'This will be the base of my shroud', was my immediate thought, and I took the role of fabric to the counter where our acquaintance was making her purchases. 'Well Lia', she said, 'what are you going to make with that gorgeous red'? I paused a moment, not sure if I was willing to talk about shrouds in a fabric shop but then thought, why not? 'I am planning to make a shroud.' A moment of silence and surprised faces; the young shop assistant looked awkward and giggled. The acquaintance exclaimed: 'What for, you look hale and hearty? You won't be needing that for a long time!' The shop manager, also within hearing, said she had heard a lot of talk in her shop but never the mention of making your own shroud! These comments turned into a delightful, light and honest conversation about death, funerals, art, and the making of shrouds—and all that within a brief encounter in a city fabric shop. I now have the fabric and it is my intention to gather a group of friends or interested people to form a creative circle where we each work on decorating our shrouds or our coffins while engaged in inspiring and uplifting conversation, likely about life and death.

Now, with the deceased person cared for and dressed or shrouded and or placed in a coffin, we can turn our attention to other funeral matters that I briefly touched on earlier.

Notification

Informing family, friends, colleagues, acquaintances, and others—is it your wish that a card be sent, or notification be made via internet, or simply a notice in the local paper? For the sending of a card, you could design one yourself or choose a design beforehand. Leave a detailed list of names, addresses and other contact details of the people you would like to be notified. You may also choose to write the death notice yourself.

Visiting and viewing

Viewing of your body at the funeral home or your place of choice provides a final opportunity for those left behind to spend time with you. This is a personal choice and for some seeing a deceased person can be confronting. However, for some people viewing can be especially important to help with the grieving process. It helps them to face the reality of death, say their goodbyes and have a quiet moment to reflect and to remember. A viewing can be part of the wake where family and friends gather with the body of the deceased before the funeral. It provides an opportunity for the sharing of memories and the celebration of their life. Consider whether you would like your body to be available for viewing; for some viewings people choose to have a closed coffin, but their loved ones are still able to spend quiet time with them. So, if it is 'yes' for a viewing, would you like the coffin open or closed? If closed, would you like a photograph of yourself displayed on top?

Transporting the body

Whatever your funeral choice, your body will need to be transferred from either the funeral home or a private dwelling to a place of service, burial ground or crematorium. For transport, a body must be well contained in a casket or coffin to keep the body and potential emissions of decay from escaping. The law requires that a body must not be visible while in transit.[163] For this reason, for most people hiring a funeral car will be the logical option. Check with a funeral director what legal requirement need to be fulfilled for the transportation of a body.

The funeral service

What services are available? What service would you like? This could be a faith-based funeral which will be held in a place of worship and supported by your faith-based community, or you may wish to have the full memorial service organised by a funeral director at a funeral home or a funeral celebrant at a place of your choice, and then again you may have a memorial and the wake at your own home. You may have family, religious or cultural traditions you wish to respect. What funeral option is the best for you will depend on your wishes, your budget and your support team.

Increasingly, people are starting to push back against the high costs of funeral services. There is the cost of hiring a venue, engaging a celebrant or funeral director, transportation, cremation or burial costs, and arranging catering services. It all adds up. The funeral industry is a business and lacks much competition or regulation, which leaves the consumer paying the huge bills, often without much choice.[164] When a funeral has not been planned, it is up to those left behind to make hard-headed financial decisions when they are emotional and grieving, which is another reason why stating your preferences well before death makes life easier for the ones left behind. You do not have to have a funeral and you could make the choice of a no-service funeral.

Merily's choice was to have a no-service funeral. From the hospice she was transferred directly to the crematorium. Her family arranged a memorial service to be held a month after her death, at a place in nature where Merily's ashes were scattered and where family and friends were given an opportunity to say a few words. After this ritual and ceremony invited family and friends gathered at Merily's home for the wake and a feast. Food and friendship went hand in hand as far as Merily was concerned, and therefore the family requested all guests to bring a plate with food to share, and indeed it was a food festive celebration of her life. Merily was an artist, and it was her wish for family and friends to choose one of her paintings which were displayed at the wake, and to make a financial donation to an artistic development project.

Whether choosing a more formal funeral service or a simple celebration of life ceremony, the following points are worth considering.

- Flowers and decorations: If you wish to have them, do you want colourful, one colour, commercially grown or from your own garden?
- Who will preside over the service, who is to speak?
- Opening prayers or remarks or a poem: Do you want any? If yes, which ones, and to be read by whom?
- What is to be said, or what special or inspirational readings, religious or other, would you like?
- Do you want lots of people involved in the funeral service? If so, what is the best way to engage them?
- Who will give the eulogy if one is to be given?

- Are individual mourners to be offered the opportunity to share memories?
- What music, hymns or songs would you like? Would you like someone to sing or play an instrument?
- What rituals would you like to be held?
- Who will be the pallbearers?
- Will you have a book for mourners to sign or write messages? If so, who will look after it, and who will keep it after the ceremony?

A wake

A wake provides the opportunity for family and friends to come together and celebrate the person that you were. A few things to consider:
- Do you want to hold a wake? Some people choose to have a wake before their death, to be able to take part in the memory sharing.
- Where would you like your wake to be held? And before or after you die?
- In either case, who will provide the food and beverages?

Consider the cost if required. Do you hire a funeral home venue, or can you accommodate the mourners at home or at a community hall? Would the local football club or RSL club be suitable? Is there a place that reflects your personality and wishes, that creates a more relaxed atmosphere and that is not time limited? Will you have the event catered or will you ask everyone to bring some food to share? Extra funds saved could be donated to a worthy cause or charity, in the same way that some people request no flowers at a funeral and ask for donations instead.

Disposing of the body

Cemetery

The most traditional style for cemetery interment is a specific burial plot, which is identified with a headstone or other monument made of granite, marble or other stone. The designs of headstone vary between elaborate and very simple. A lawn cemetery is where burial is under lawn and each grave is marked with a small commemorative plaque. A natural or 'green' burial is a funeral and burial which endeavours to make as little impact upon the environment as possible and ensures that the body wrapping is decomposable. The burial site is in a special designated green cemetery or in natural bushland with little or no marking, although there could be a planting of a tree, flowers, or placing of a natural rock.

Each of these different styles of cemetery have their costs for opening and closing of the grave with earth-moving equipment, installation and removal of a lowering device, registration fees, and re-grading and sodding of lawn and placement of other materials used at the graveside during the funeral.

Cremation

At a cremation, the body will be brought to the oven area. On top of the casket there is fire-resistant stone with an identification number and outside the oven there is a tag, both for the identification of body. The body will be rolled via trolley into the oven and burned at an extremely high temperature. The ashes will be collected in an urn.

Aquamation

Alkaline hydrolysis, also called aquamation or biocremation, is a new alternative for the disposing of the body and considered to be more environmentally friendly than traditional cremation. Aquamation's website states: 'Alkaline hydrolysis is a non-burn process that is completely automated. Alkaline hydrolysis uses a combination of flowing water, high temperature and alkalinity to accelerate the natural course of tissue and chemical breakdown.'[165] All that remains after this process are the bones, which are ground up and placed in an urn as 'ashes' and returned to the family. In Australia, this process is available only in New South Wales, Queensland and Victoria at present.[166]

Composting burial

Another environmentally friendly alternative for the disposing of the body is a composting burial, also known as 'natural organic reduction' composting burial, an inventive idea by US researcher, Katrina Spade. According to an article in *The Conversation*, the body is placed 'into a vessel containing a mix of soil, wood chips, straw and alfalfa. As decomposition begins, microbial activity creates heat. This speeds things up and eliminates germs from the mix' and over a period of about four weeks converts human remains into soil.[167] For further details see the website of Recompose. It is the first human composting funeral home, based in Washington USA. Human composting is not legal in Australia … yet.

Final considerations

- Notification and finalising of paperwork, the closing of bank accounts after your death (ensure you leave good instructions behind in your will).
- Dividing up personal belongings such as art and jewellery as this will hopefully relieve stresses and disagreements. You may choose to distribute these items before your death or discuss your decisions before death or simply leave instructions in your will.
- Clearing out of final personal 'stuff': If you have not done this before death, ensure you have informed your family what you want done with your personal belongings such as diaries, old correspondence, etc.

I agree, it is a long list of matters to consider around death and organising a funeral. Consider your options, work out what you want and find out whether what you would like is available in your State or Territory. Check out the various costs involved regarding disposal of your body, the cost of a service or a funeral director, a wake, transport of body, home or a funeral parlour, and all the logistics involved. It makes the tasks for your loved ones much easier, saves a lot of stress and likely a lot of money. Have a conversation with a funeral director and find out what services they offer. Gain an awareness of what to look out for, how not to be pressured into making decisions or to spend more than your budget, as they do tend to upsell. Make sure the funeral director is upfront and answers your questions truthfully. You need straight answers. You have the luxury of time for consideration if you plan now. If your family or friends are making these enquiries and decisions after you have died, there will be time pressures that may force their hand to accept a particular option, which might not be to your wishes.

Planning and arranging in advance will be of great relief to those who are dealing with your affairs on your death. Advanced planning enables you to consider the various options, and personalise the event, and it helps your family to know what you would like and what your preferences are. It is in a way a last caring gift to your family as you have made it less difficult and less complicated during an emotional time of grieving. You know your own circumstances best; your children may be living interstate or overseas and therefore not able to immediately start planning a funeral.

Document your wishes, and remember to tell your family where they can find all documentation: have your will, your advance care directive, and your funeral plans together in the one folder. And when your funeral and end of life ceremony has been considered, planned, and documented, feel the pleasure of being organised, get on and get about, and enjoy the rest of your life!

For me, having thoughts and making some plans for my funeral was not a chore, although it required a bit of courage as well as taking some risks, since my choices may seem to some people to be less traditional. My husband and children engaged in the conversations and are pleased and relieved that a huge chunk of planning for my funeral has been taken care of. There will still likely be plenty of matters for them to consider, organise and sort out when the time comes. You may also find you need a bit of courage to tackle the planning of your funeral and for that we will have our final conversation on having courage and taking risks, in the next chapter of this book.

The Facts of Life

*That you were born
and you will die.
That you will sometimes love enough
and sometimes not.
That you will lie
if only to yourself.
That you will get tired.
That you will learn most from the situations
you did not choose.
That there will be some things that move you
more than you can say.
That you will live
that you must be loved.
That will avoid questions most urgent in need of
your attention.
That you began as the fusion of a sperm and an egg
of two people who were once strangers and may well still be.
That life isn't fair.
That life is sometimes good
and sometimes even better than good.
That life is often not so good.
That life is real
and if you can survive it, well,
survive it well
With love and art
and meaning given where meaning is scarce.*

That you will learn to live with regret.
That you will learn to live with respect.
That the structures that constrict you
may not be permanently restricting.
That you will probably be okay.
That you must accept change
before you die
but you will die anyway.
So you might as well live
and you might as well love.
You might as well love.
You might as well love.

Padraig O Tuama[168]

Resources

A how-to guide for making funeral arrangements: https://www.funeralwise.com/plan/how_to/

Choice: 'Lifting the lid on funerals.' 2016. Examines your funeral options, and the impact on your pocket and the planet. https://www.choice.com.au/health-and-body/healthy-ageing/ageing-and-retirement/articles/diy-funerals-and-coffins

Choice: 1800 069 552

Funeral Consumers Alliance. 2020. 'Green burial, an environmentally friendly choice.' https://funerals.org/wp-content/uploads/2020/11/2020-11-14-green-burial.pdf brochure. Note that this is a US based site, so some of the information may not be relevant in Australia.

Funeral Directors Australia: www.funeraldirectorsaustralia.com.au

Gathered Here: Funeral planning check list. https://www.gatheredhere.com.au/funeral-planning-checklist-australia/

Gathered Here. 'Green Funerals in Australia.' https://www.gatheredhere.com.au/green-funerals-australia/#:~:text=Green%20Coffins%20and%20Caskets,and%20sustainable%20to%20the%20environment.

Natural Death Advocacy Network (NDAN): www.ndan.com.au

Heather Wiseman. 2016. 'Preparing a loved one's body for a family-led funeral.' https://palliativecare.org.au/how-to-prepare-a-loved-ones-body-for-burial-and-have-a-family-led-funeral/

Tender Funerals Australia . Tender Funerals is a not-for-profit funeral service model that aims to ensure that all Australians can have access to meaningful and affordable funerals. https://tenderfunerals.com.au/

CHAPTER 11

Courage to Change: To Live, Age and Die Well

Courage is what it takes to be fully human. It's what pushes us to survive the daily navigations between the known and the not-known; to deal with the inevitable; to create useful distinctions between what we can change and what we cannot. It is what will allow us to go into our own particular versions of hell. It is what will give us the strength and the grace to re-emerge, and still find life worth living.
— STEPHANIE DOWRICK, *FORGIVENESS AND OTHER ACTS OF LOVE*

Each of these last ten chapters introduced a theme around ageing well, topics for you to explore, tease out, reflect upon, and to seriously consider. Each chapter was written to encourage you to engage in open and honest conversation with yourself and with others, family, friends and peers. These more in-depth conversations about getting older are not your everyday chats you may have had in passing with family or friends. The topics outlined are not an 'if this happens, you do that' formula, they contain no expert advice. As individuals we will all age differently and we will all have our individual needs, challenges, opportunities and wishes. Each chapter includes questions for you to ponder seriously, and no answers are provided. There are no 'right' answers, no one-size-fits-all in ageing, and there are often no easy answers. It is for you to seek the answers which are applicable to you, because *you* are the expert on your life and you know the circumstances you live in at present.

Are you content with the status quo of your life, or are changes required? How does change make you feel? Did you feel uncomfortable or even fearful when you read and considered each of the different and intense topics under discussion? Did some of it strike a chord with you? Have you been able to talk about ageing, living and dying, or do they remain uncomfortable or taboo conversations? Mark Manson, the author of *The Subtle Art of Not Giving a F*ck*, recognises this reluctance and has the following ideas about its cause. He calls it 'Manson's law of avoidance': 'The more something threatens your identity, the more you will avoid it. That means the more something threatens to change how you view yourself, how successful/unsuccessful you believe yourself to be, how well you see yourself living up to your values, the more you will avoid ever getting around to doing it. There's a certain comfort that comes with knowing how you fit in the world. Anything that shakes up that comfort [such as considering your ageing future]—even if it could potentially make your life better—is inherently scary'.[169]

'Old age ain't no place for sissies,' Bette Davis once said, and 'Ageing is not for the weak' is a chapter title in Ken Hillman's book *A Good Life To The End*.[170] Ageing is hard, ageing is tough *but* it can be—and is for many—enormously rewarding. The challenge is that there does not seem to be a 'just right' balance. Your mind and soul remain active, alert and, for some, 'forever young' although the physical body is experiencing decline. There can be an experience of bizarre contradiction and discombobulation, an imbalance. How to age, pursue living life, and die well in a meaningful manner? Does this take courage—why would you need courage?

The word courage came to English via the French *coeur*, from the Latin *cor*, meaning 'heart'.[171] Shelly Francis, in her book *The Courage Way*, speaks of 'fortitude' as another word for courage, and recommends

COURAGE TO CHANGE: TO LIVE, AGE AND DIE WELL

we 'combine them both and think "strength of heart"'.[172] It will take courage and fortitude, this 'strength of heart', to overcome our fears and make the required changes as we age.

This chapter is about courage: courage and a willingness to take some risks when bringing about change. When you courageously and frankly engage with each topic under discussion and face ageing with your head as well as your heart, it becomes less challenging and easier to address. After reflective journaling on the questions and by exploring the options and alternatives you may have gained insight into what ageing means for you now and into your future. Atul Gawande in his book *Being Mortal* describes two kinds of courage we need in ageing and in sickness:

> The first is the courage to confront the reality of mortality—the courage to seek out the truth of what is to be feared and what is to be hoped. Such courage is difficult enough. We have many reasons to shrink from it. But even more daunting is the second kind of courage—the courage to act on the truth we find. The problem is that the wise course is so frequently unclear. For a long while, I thought that this was simply because of uncertainty. When it is hard to know what will happen, it is hard to know what to do. But the challenge, I have come to see, is more fundamental than that. One has to decide whether one's fears or one's hopes are what should matter most.[173]

Your understanding of ageing, your preparedness and willingness to take on the responsibility for your ageing future will help to ease your burden and the burden on your family members who may otherwise find themselves in the position of having to make crucial decisions with little time for thought or research, in a time of crisis and likely with little understanding of ageing related matters.

You are a very courageous person if you have come this far in reading and working through this book. Each chapter has persuaded you to look in the mirror, see yourself in life at this moment while also considering your ageing future. In chapter one, Home, Belonging and Community, you reflected on what home means to you and what gives you that sense of belonging.

For Annette, home is in her local community in the UK where she has lived and worked for most of her life; however, she has decided to immigrate to Australia where both of her children live. With them she has that true sense of belonging. It is with her children and grandchildren that she wants to be in her ageing years. Annette had to make a choice and she needed to do this early (while still healthy and active), and she chose carefully. Janis Dietz in her book *Yes, You Can* wrote: 'Remember, you always have a choice' and here Dietz quotes Abraham Lincoln: 'the choices you make today will affect the rest of your life; so make them carefully. The responsibility is yours, and the choice is yours.'[174] Annette appreciated her choices, and realised that it would take courage to relocate, create a new home and find a place to belong. It was not an easy decision and it tugged at her heart strings—courage was needed. Annette shared her sense of relief when she said 'yes' to joining her children, which enabled her to make plans for her future in Australia and move on with living her life.

As Shelly Francis writes in *The Courage Way*: 'Different circumstances call for different ways of being courageous', and she lists four kinds of courage: 'physical, moral, social and creative'.[175] I have witnessed and heard many stories from clients and conversation participants about managing their chronic illness, living with cancer or a disability, or having constant discomfort or pain, situations that are in some cases part of the realities of ageing. Physical courage is needed to show up each new day and face the challenges of living with a debilitating illness. 'I need to simply get on with living life,' said my friend Merily who was living with cancer, 'I wish to make the most of each and every day I have left.' It takes courage and commitment, when living with physical or mental illness, to make choices on how best to live life each day. Double courage is needed, in my opinion, if you live with a chronic illness while you care for your partner who has health problems or lives with dementia, and this scenario is not at all uncommon.

'Ageism is a global challenge' and 'ageism affects how we think, feel and act towards others and ourselves based on age', reports the World Health Organisation.[176] Standing up to and tackling ageism requires courage: courage and strength of heart to speak out to injustice as individuals and as a collective, which Francis calls moral courage: 'Moral courage is about the righting of wrongs, taking the risk to speak truth to power, to demand change and face the consequences.'[177] Numerous 'isms' are entrenched in our societies and ageism is one of them. Speaking out against ageism on your own can be challenging and by joining with others you have a stronger voice. As an individual you can take personal responsibility and make the pledge provided by EveryAGE Counts, an advocacy campaign against ageism: 'I stand for a world without ageism where all people of all ages are valued and respected and their contributions are acknowledged. I commit to speak out and take action to ensure older people can participate on equal terms with others in all aspects of life.'[178] After I made the pledge, I received a reply email that included several suggestions about what we can do to challenge ageism. One suggestion is to start *a conversation* (which we are having now) and check out our assumptions and beliefs around ageism.

Money is an important component of our ageing years; a lack of funds while trying to meet the required needs of ageing well in a humane manner can cause a lot of angst. Pascal mentioned being unsure of his and his partner's ageing future, counts on his children's support and feels to be in a rather vulnerable position. Heather and Amy are finding themselves in a similarly vulnerable and financially exposed situation and they do worry about their future. It already takes courage and frugality to meet the costs of day-to-day living and it will need courage to trust that all will be well and provided for as ageing needs change.

Our conversation about care and care support highlighted some of the challenges, neglect and poor care outcomes identified by the Royal

Commission into Aged Care Quality and Safety. The recommendations handed down are to encourage governments and institutions to come up with what Francis calls 'creative courage' to bring about positive change in care provision.

> [Creative courage] is the courage to come up with creative solutions, to create community, to create meaning from challenges, to create new visions and symbols that other people can rally around, and to create change that moves us forward in our humanity. Sometimes creative courage means instigating change from within the institutions and organizations that need to be called back to their original intention to serve the greater good.[179]

As older people we need to be courageous, to speak out and play a role in positively supporting these institutions and organisations to bring about the changes required to ensure safe and high-quality care for all older Australians. Further, it requires positive and creative courage as an initiator to play a role in providing good neighbourly, caring support within our communities. I admire all of those who care for a loved one at home, for their love, courage and the sacrifices they make. It takes a lot of love and courage to be there 24 hours a day, week in and week out. How can we as neighbours provide a little extra support? Not every older person has a choice in how they want to live in their final years and, for people like Anne who now lives in residential care and is dependent on others for care, it takes huge courage to face each new day. It also takes courage to be patient and to accept help and support from others as we age.

Making new social connections as you get older is not always easy; for this you may need a good dose of social courage. 'We exhibit social courage when we risk being vulnerable for the sake of relating to others with authentic presence. It means overcoming shame and risking loss, grief, embarrassment, sorrow, or disappointment for the possibility of love, joy, happiness, and connection.'[180] It takes courage to attend a group meeting where you may not have met the other participants before. Initially you may feel vulnerable in sharing your personal stories, and it will take time to build trust and make a connection. This was the case for Jody, a conversation participant—as a self-described 'private person' she preferred not to talk much about herself. Jody somewhat reluctantly engaged in the Social Circle activity as outlined in chapter six: The Importance of Social Connections. In all the conversation groups I run I emphasise that there are no 'must do' things; if you do not wish to engage in an activity you pass and you share if you wish to share. After the activity in the group sharing, Jody briefly spoke about her three furry friends as very important companions and did not comment further. The following week, Jody referred to the activity and quietly shared how difficult it had been for her. She disclosed how challenging it is for her to make new social connections since her retirement from work and how scared, lonely and sad she was feeling. Jody showed huge social courage in her willingness to show her vulnerability in sharing her personal difficulties about making new social connections.

After her fall in Tasmania, Jacki courageously faced the realities of ageing. As she said: 'my injury stopped me in my track, my reality had shifted, and change was required. It forced my hand, so to speak'. After her initial shock and recovery, and with the support of health professionals, Jacki put her life back in order. She considered all options regarding housing, pondered the pros and cons of downsizing or right-sizing, and decided to renovate her home so she could live independently. Jacki is a realist and is determined to age well at home in her community. More than likely you know the benefits of moving to a more manageable house or being closer to family and friends, medical support or community facilities. Moving is challenging: it means having to let go of your home and decades of collected belongings with all their attached memories. Moving is stressful, but it can be an exciting experience; it will take a huge amount of courage to let go of what was and embrace the new.

Living life with meaning and purpose, and with the awareness of our mortality, is work filled with courage. As we age and experience an increase in vulnerability and need for others, courage is even more beneficial. We will use this human quality to listen to the inner voice of our true self, reflect upon its message, and engage and learn from others so that—together—we can discover and engage with the complexities of our ageing future. It is the enjoyable, informative and difficult conversations we have with others that will help us to overcome fear and courageously make decisions to find ongoing meaning in life as we age.

One of those courageous conversations is around making decisions for our end of life care. What are your needs and what are your preferences? Who do you need to have this conversation with, and would you have the courage to talk about life and death? If it is difficult for you to talk about dying and death, consider a person who could help you with these conversations. I shared with you the story of my goddaughter Lucy and her courageous journey of living with cancer, her strength of heart and the love she showed her family, friends and others who knew her in the brave way she had her end of life conversations and spoke about her wishes for living and dying. For Merily, this was not so easy; she struggled with this whole 'dying thing', and preferred 'to just die in my sleep'. However, she did gather up her courage, prepared her advance care directive and had the difficult conversations with her loved ones. It is not an easy journey but it was a moving end of life journey Merily and her loved ones undertook together. And although I am able and comfortable to talk about dying and death now, who knows how courageous I will be when my time comes?

At a recent workshop I had some flyers on the table to promote a couple of conversations on end of life planning and a conversation on planning for your funeral. One woman, who shared that she was 70, looked at the flyer and stated: 'This is not for me!' I was curious and asked her what she meant. 'Not there yet, and not my problem', was her initial answer. In talking a bit further, she revealed that she felt uncomfortable and scared when talking about death and dying. 'Funerals are too expensive, I can't afford that, my kids can sort this out when the time comes'—although she acknowledged that she did not want to burden her children with the responsibility of having to consider care options and medical intervention, or incur funeral costs. We talked some more about sharing her thoughts with others, keeping an open mind and possibly making enquiries and exploring options. The woman considered this for a moment, asked more about the topics of conversation, and decided to take a flyer. I suggested she could bring a friend for support. It takes courage to think about and plan for a 'good' death and funeral.

For each of our conversations, courage is needed and demonstrated. Life never goes according to plan; we cannot control life—or ageing, for that matter. There is no linear pathway to our ultimate death. It will be a different experience for each one of us; life happens: the good, the bad and the ugly. We can only work with what comes our way and we may have to simply accept the things we cannot control and play the cards we have been dealt. There is no 'softly, softly' approach to facing increasing frailty. Your lived experience and the stories we have heard about declining health and decreasing abilities are a reality check. It could be a frightening and overwhelming journey and courage is needed.

What are your concerns? Is there something you can do to prepare yourself? Consider what you need courage for. Will it be for dealing with declining health, your changing looks and failing strength, your grief around loss of family and friends, of loss of your home and the freedom of your car and driver's license, of loss of social activities (because of fear of going out at night) and independence? And will you need courage to make amends with your past, to heal old hurts or resentments?

In the words of Liz Evans, 'Courage is shaped by consciousness and risks. Finding courage means making deliberated decisions and choices, and taking purposeful actions in the face of frightening or painful circumstances in order to effect change for the better.'[181]

Undertake courage with a dose of grace and do not go it alone, ageing is not a solo act. We are on this journey with others, we are part of a community. And here is where these conversations with others in a group work so well as we encourage and stimulate each other to consider the necessary changes. We find and work with courage together. Courageous ageing matters and makes a difference to your feelings of empowerment and wellbeing. Gathering and working together is what Francis would call 'creative courage leading to collective courage',[182] which is working and growing together to bring about change. To live and age wholeheartedly is a strategic direction from the heart, and it takes minute by minute courage.

So, looking toward the future courageously, how do we move forward? I believe it is the Australian poet Michael Leunig who provides us some guidance on how to get there. I encourage you to read Leunig's poem 'How to get there' in his book *The Travelling Leunig* or on his website: www.leunig.com.au. I would add, you get where you wish to go just by taking one courageous step at a time!

Activity: Reflections

The courage to act on the truth we find, as described by Gawande earlier, means taking risks.

As we face the future, we have a choice—not everyone believes this, but it is true! Even if you are not sure, consider:
- Embrace risks and new adventures: determine your own pathway.
- Explore the risk of staying where or as you are, or take on new challenges and adventures and move on to whatever comes next.
- Where and how do you want to live and where and how do you want to die?
- What would you do if you had courage and were not afraid?
- What if?

'Imagination is everything. It is the preview of life's coming attractions,' Albert Einstein is reported as saying.[183]

Activity: thinking outside the box

Let's contemplate our vision for the next stage in our lives and by doing this let's think outside the box: envision being the person you aspire to be into your ageing future.

- What would you be doing if you were ten times more courageous in the next part of your life than you were in the first part?
- What would you do?
- Where would you be living?
- Who would be part of your life?
- What would be 'just right' ageing for you?
- Add to the activity from chapter eight, the review of your life lived. How would you answer this question: What are you most proud of doing during these last 10-odd years?

CONCLUSION

On Your Way

To begin your journey into the next stage of our life, here's some advice from Martin Luther King: 'Take the first step in faith. You don't have to see the whole staircase, just take the first step'. Be adventurous! Let's start with one final artistic activity that helps with emotional and physical release. Have some artistic fun and play.

Artistic activity

Get a large sheet of strong paper or a big canvas and some acrylic paints. Use your hands, fingers or, if need be, a paint brush. Play a favourite piece of music that makes you feel strong and joyful, such as Beethoven's 'Ode to Joy', Helen Reddy singing 'I am Woman', Holst's 'Jupiter' or whatever choice of music gets your heart singing. Let your fingers do the dancing with paint on paper, but do not overdo it with too many colours or it will all turn a muddy brown! Be daring and take some risks with shapes and colour combinations. Move your fingers, hands, feet and body to the sounds of the music and enjoy! Afterwards, reflect on the activity: how did you feel as you tuned into the music? How did different sounds or your different responses to the music influence your choice of colour, of shape?

Finally ...

The writing of this conversation series into a book was, for me, a step requiring courage. There were many moments of uncertainty, doubt about my ability, and feelings of vulnerability. How do I write a book on 'ageing well' that will be of interest to many people, and that is supportive and encouraging, that motivates the readers to bring about the changes required for them to age well—but that, on the other hand, does not preach or suggest that I have all the answers? I am a strong believer in 'practicing what I preach' and so, while writing, I reflected honestly on my life and considered my ageing future. I like to make sense of my world and make plans, which likely highlights my need of keeping things in control! Change is inevitable and can be positive, but it requires vulnerability and the willingness to reflect and to take some risks. The following words from Richard Leider and David Shapiro sum up my experience fittingly:

> Ultimately, the place we are looking for is a place somewhere within us. We must journey inward as well as outward to find our place in the world. Like those intrepid explorers of old who sailed off to *terra incognita*, we too must be willing to venture into uncharted waters. We must be willing to explore all the regions of our own world—our internal world—about which the maps provide no information. And to succeed in our quest, we must do more than merely peer over the edge of those maps, we must venture into the unknown as well.[184]

I had not written a book before and it was an interesting and stimulating mission. I considered my 'what ifs' and pondered how I would address certain matters. I have made and will make changes to the way I live and work, and I will continue to deliberate and make choices about my ageing and dying future.

It has been a bonus that, after the initial coronavirus pandemic lockdown, I was able to resume facilitating in-person ageing-well conversations within community groups. In these conversations with others I had several 'aha' moments, suggestions made by participants which would be useful for me to consider. In addition, I have made a start with my own changes, such as taking an audit of the areas in my home which need attention to ensure I am able to age well and safely in place. I have had plans drawn up for bathroom modifications that includes removal of the big bath, installation of a level-floor walk-in shower with support rails, and have helped develop a safer, level access option to modify the pathway from our front door to the street. I have prepared, discussed, and officially signed and distributed my advance care directive and, in conversation and consultation with my family, I have documented my wishes for my future care and funeral. Having said all this, I am aware that it is good to review my advance care directive at times to ensure my wishes and choices remain up to date. Further, the ongoing in-person conversations in communities will ensure that I keep learning and stay up to date with relevant information around ageing well in the community.

I found 'living life with meaning' and 'having courage to make changes' the most challenging topics to reflect and act on. How can I live life being true to myself, what do I care about? What is my work? Where am I still able to courageously contribute within my community and help it ripple out into the wider world? I am passionate about supporting people to live and die well and I am considering options on how to best further this work. Of course, there are the uncertainties, and it requires courage to overcome niggling fears about my confidence and ability to do this work. Nevertheless, living life to the fullest requires what I spoke about in my opening words: living and working with an open heart, an open mind and the willingness to bring about change. Openness of heart and mind is a commitment to explore new opportunities and to be open to new ideas and new ways of doing.

Ageing sneaks up on us, being 21 or 45 was not that long ago and here I am, here you are aged 65, 73, 82 … and it is likely we have been slow in accepting the changes. Now is the time to reflect on and consider the next stage of your life. Gather and connect with others for a conversation. The objective of ageing well can be too challenging or frightening to achieve alone; it needs family, friends, peers and our communities to help us move forward. As Parker Palmer writes: we need a 'community of support ... people who share our failures and successes, our hopes and our fears, people who can help us find the courage to take the next step'.[185]

Consider this as both my sincere invitation to you to consider options, reflect and reminisce, and the sharing of experiences as a gift to all. Chats with others can be very enlivening for all who engage. Sharing our stories helps us to identify the common threads of experience in each of our stories. You will be surprised at how interesting your life events and stories may be to others, and how you will find that you will benefit from hearing about other people's lives and their thoughts on the various topics discussed. Each of our stories has value and adds to our understanding of ageing. The conversations with others will provoke our thinking about the 'what ifs' and they will trigger our tears as well as shared laughter and camaraderie.

So, prepare for your future years. Start talking about ageing, about end of life and your ultimate death. As we face the reality of our ageing future, we have a responsibility, and we make our choices. The choices we make today will influence the quality of our future ageing days. Use your imagination, and dare to grow by informing yourself and support others on their journey. I wish you well.

Activity: planting the future

Here is one last activity: I invite you to buy some seeds and to plant them into some rich soil, either in the garden or in a pot to have inside the house, perhaps on a windowsill. Give these seeds a name, such as 'courage', 'inspiration', 'change', 'new life', or whatever is most suited to your future dreams. If you would like to see an idea or vision of what it means for you to age well grow, you will need to water these seeds occasionally! You can plant an idea for making change OR you can leave possibilities unattended. The choice is yours!

Don't just dream—plant a seed

*Though I do not believe that a plant will
spring up where no seed has been,
I have great faith in a seed.
Convince me that you have a seed there and
I am prepared to expect wonders.*

Henry David Thoreau, *The Succession of Forest Trees*

Acknowledgements

My sincere gratitude and huge THANK YOU to:

All the extraordinary people within the community, my friendship circle and the conversation participants who gave me their trust and who so generously shared their personal stories with me for this book. Your lived experiences have contributed to highlight the challenges and opportunities of ageing.

Colleagues from The Australian Centre for Social Innovation for enabling me to work alongside you on projects related to 'Ageing Well'. Kerry Jones for your trust and belief in this conversation series and to Burgh O'Brien, Leanne McPhee and Barbara Binns for your advice, debrief and support with the initial conversations and our discussions on alternative housing options. The conversation series is happening in the community and this in turn led me to writing this book. Thank you all for your friendship.

Friend and mentor Dr Victoria Cornell for the great conversations we have had on all matters related to ageing. I very much appreciate your support with the reading of early draft versions and your comments, feedback, and suggestions, all very helpful and informative. Thank you for sharing your knowledge and expertise, and for your encouragement and belief in me.

Margaret McDonell, my highly skilled editor and advisor on all things book related, I appreciate your patience and all your valuable contributions. Thank you for the sharing of your lived experiences. It is wonderful how our singing in choir together lead to you editing this book.

Myrana Wahlqvist being my neighbourly editor, proof reading anything even slightly 'official'. You are a magician with words and to keeping me within the required word count.

Kathy Williams and Fallon Hardy and their teams from the Office for Ageing Well for believing in the conversation series and the book. Thank you for all your support.

Sanne Kerssens for her delightful illustration on the front cover!

Ann Calvert for the final proofreading. I appreciate you reading my work with fresh eyes and providing valuable comments.

Rommie Corso from Hardshell Publishing for your kind support, expertise and creative skills to shape this book into its final form for publication.

To all my dear and supportive friends for your willingness to listen to my never-ending stories about getting older, the challenges, the opportunities and the joys! I look forward to sharing a realistic and delightful ageing future with the lot of you!

My family: husband Graeme, children and children-in-law: Josine, Briston, Luke, Hannah and Elja for your love, encouragement and support. Graeme for his skills, knowledge and patience when I became challenged by anything word-processing and computer program related. My grandchildren Arian, Flynn, Felix, Marlow and Anouk for joy, laughter and keeping me 'young'. It is you with whom I share my lived experience and with whom I look forward to sharing my ageing future.

References

Advance Care Planning Australia. 2015. 'Advance Care Planning 1: Starting the conversation'. Video. https://www.youtube.com/watch?v=QagbgTYCtMY

Advance Care Planning Australia. 2021. https://www.advancecareplanning.org.au/

Aged Care Quality and Safety Commission. 2021. Becoming an approved aged care provider. https://www.agedcarequality.gov.au/providers/becoming-approved-aged-care-provider

Aged Care Quality and Safety Commission. 2020. *Guidance for Applicants Seeking Approval to Provide Aged Care*. Booklet. https://www.agedcarequality.gov.au/sites/default/files/media/guidance_for_applicants_seeking_approval_to_provide_aged_care_0.pdf

The AGEncy Project. 2021. www.agencycohcom.org

Albom, M. 1997. *Tuesdays with Morrie.* Hodder Headline Australia, Rydalmere, NSW.

Applewhite, A. 2017. 'Let's end ageism'. TED2017 video. https://www.ted.com/talks/ashton_applewhite_let_s_end_ageism

Applewhite, A. 2019. *This Chair Rocks: A manifesto against ageism.* Celadon Books, New York.

Aquamation International. 2021. Aquamation. http://www.aquamationindustries.com/what-is-alkaline-hydrolysis

Australian Broadcasting Corporation. 2019. 'Retraining won't keep older workers from choosing to retire'. https://www.abc.net.au/news/2019-11-20/retraining-wont-keep-older-workers-from-choosing-to-retire/11720482

Australian Bureau of Statistics. 2011. Retirement and retirement intentions. Cat no: 6238.0. ABS, Canberra. https://www.abs.gov.au/statistics/labour/employment-and-unemployment/retirement-and-retirement-intentions-australia/latest-release#:~:text=55%25%20of%20people%20over%2055,to%20retire%20is%2065.5%20years

Australian Bureau of Statistics. 2016. Disability, ageing and carers, Australia: Summary of findings, 2015. Cat no: 4430.0. ABS, Canberra. https://www.abs.gov.au/ausstats/abs@.nsf/Lookup/4430.0main+features302015

Australian Bureau of Statistics. 2017. Census of population and housing: Reflecting Australia – Stories from the census, 2016. Cat no: 2071.0. https://www.abs.gov.au/ausstats/abs@.nsf/Lookup/by%20Subject/2071.0~2016~Main%20Features~Ageing%20Population~14

The Australian Centre for Social Innovation. 2017. Investing in systemic impacts to improve end of life outcomes. Summary report. https://www.tacsi.org.au/wp-content/uploads/2018/07/Systemic-Impact-in-End-of-Life_report-updated-02.07.2018.pdf

The Australian Centre for Social Innovation. 2018. Future directions to support ageing well. Report prepared for the South Australian Government Office for the Ageing. https://www.sahealth.sa.gov.au/wps/wcm/connect/Public+Content/SA+Health+Internet/About+Us/Department+for+Health+and+Wellbeing/Office+for+Ageing+Well/Resources/Resources+about+ageing+well

Australian Doula College. 2020. https://www.australiandoulacollege.com.au

Australian Government Organ and Tissue Authority. 2021. 'Register as a donor today'. https://donatelife.gov.au/register-donor-today

Australian Government, Department of Health. 2019. Advance care planning. https://www.health.gov.au/health-topics/palliative-care/planning-your-palliative-care/advance-care-planning

Australian Government, Department of Health. 2021. Budget delivers $17.7 billion for once a generation change to aged care in Australia. https://www.health.gov.au/news/budget-delivers-177-billion-for-once-in-a-generation-change-to-aged-care-in-australia

Australian Government, Department of Social Services. 2019. Age pension. https://www.dss.gov.au/seniors/benefits-payments/age-pension

References

Australian Housing and Urban Research Institute (AHURI). 2021. Better supporting older Australians to age in place. https://www.ahuri.edu.au/research/ahuri-briefs/better-supporting-older-australians-to-age-in-place

Australian Human Rights Commission. 2019. Age Discrimination: exposing the hidden barrier for mature age workers (2010). https://humanrights.gov.au/our-work/age-discrimination/publications/age-discrimination-exposing-hidden-barrier-mature-age

Australian Institute of Health and Welfare. 2018. Older Australians at a glance. https://www.aihw.gov.au/reports/older-people/older-australia-at-a-glance/contents/demographics-of-older-australians

Australian Institute of Health and Welfare. 2019. Social isolation and loneliness. https://www.aihw.gov.au/reports/australias-welfare/social-isolation-and-loneliness

Australian Institute of Health and Welfare. 2020. Housing assistance in Australia 2020. https://www.aihw.gov.au/reports/housing-assistance/housing-assistance-in-australia-2020/contents/priority-groups-and-waiting-lists#wait-times

Australian Institute of Health and Welfare. 2021. Interfaces between aged care and health systems in Australia – where do older Australians die? https://www.gen-agedcaredata.gov.au/www_aihwgen/media/2021-Interfaces-reports/Interfaces-between-the-aged-care-and-health-systems-in-Australia-where-do-older-Australians-die.pdf

Automobility. 2021. Road rules for wheelchair users. https://automobility.com.au/road-rules-for-wheelchair-users

Barnes, S.F. 2011. Third age: The golden years of adulthood. *California Booming*. San Diego State University. http://calbooming.sdsu.edu/documents/TheThirdAge.pdf

The Benevolent Society. 2017. The drivers of ageism. Summary Report. www.benevolent.org.au

Bound Alberti. F. 2019. *A Biography of Loneliness: The history of an emotion*. Oxford University Press. Oxford UK.

Brenton, M. 2010. Potential benefits of cohousing for older people. A literature review. *Elderwoman*. http://www.elderwoman.org/potential_cohousing_benefits.pdf

Brodsky, J. Grey, F. & Sinclair, S. 2018. 'For Australians to have a choice of growing old at home, here is what needs to change'. *The Conversation.* https://theconversation.com/for-australians-to-have-the-choice-of-growing-old-at-home-here-is-what-needs-to-change-91488

Brown, B. 2020. 'COVID-19 puts a squeeze on older Australians' finances'. *Financial Review.* https://www.afr.com/wealth/personal-finance/covid-19-puts-squeeze-on-older-australians-finances-20200406-p54hgn

Browne. K. 2020. What to do when someone dies: A helpful checklist of the necessary processes when someone close to you passes away. *Choice.* https://www.choice.com.au/health-and-body/healthy-ageing/ageing-and-retirement/articles/what-to-do-when-someone-dies

Buckley, A. 2019. Pushing up the daisies workshop. Blog. https://www.ourfamilycelebrant.com.au/category/pushing-up-daisies-workshop/

Buettner, D. 2016. Power 9: Reverse engineering longevity. https://www.bluezones.com/2016/11/power-9/

Butler, M. 2015. *Advanced Australia: The politics of ageing.* Melbourne University Press, Carlton, Vic.

Cameron, J. 1995. *The Artist Way.* Pan Books, London.

Carter, C. 2017. *How to Handle a Toxic Relationship.* The Greater Good Science Center. https://greatergood.berkeley.edu/article/item/how_to_handle_a_toxic_relationship

Centers for Disease Control and Prevention. Morbidity and Mortality. Nonfatal Bathroom Injuries Among Persons Aged > 15 years, United States 2008. *Weekly Report,* 10 June 2011 / 60 (22), 729–33. https://www.cdc.gov/mmwr/preview/mmwrhtml/mm6022a1.htm

Centre for Ageing Better. 2019. The state of ageing in 2019: Adding life to our years. https://www.ageing-better.org.uk/sites/default/files/2019-11/The-State-of-Ageing-2019-Adding-life-to-our-years.pdf

Centre for Excellence in Universal Design. 2020. *What is Universal Design.* Dublin, Ireland. http://universaldesign.ie/What-is-Universal-Design/

Cohousing Australia. 2021. Cohousing Architecture Australia. https://cohousing.com.au/

Collaborative Housing. 2019. The Shedders. https://www.collaborativehousing.org.au/stories-the-shedders

References

Connect Victoria Park. 2021. https://www.connectvictoriapark.org/

Coorey, P. & McIlroy, T. 2021. 'PM mulls aged care tax'. Financial Review._ https://www.afr.com/politics/federal/pm-mulls-aged-care-tax-20210301-p576m8

Cottam, Hilary. 2018. *Radical Help: How we can remake the relationships between us and revolutionise the welfare state.* Virago. London.

Dawson, E., 2019. The economic impacts of ageism. Speech to the COTA Australia National Policy Forum. https://percapita.org.au/2019/06/17/speech-the-economic-impacts-of-ageism

De Campo, J., Jones, K., McPhee, L. & Vanstone, C. 2021. *The Future of Home.* The Australian Centre for Social Innovation, Adelaide. https://tacsi.org.au/future-of-home

Dietz, J. 2000. *Yes, You Can: Go beyond physical adversity and live life to its fullest.* Demos Medical, New York.

Dowrick, S. 1997. *Forgiveness and Other Acts of Love.* Penguin, Ringwood, Vic.

Dowrick, S. 2010. *Seeking the Sacred: Transforming our view of ourselves and one another.* Allen & Unwin, Crows Nest, NSW.

Durrett, C. 2009. *The Senior Cohousing Handbook: A community approach to independent living.* New Society, Gabriola Island, BC, Canada.

Ecoburbia. 2018. Creating more sustainable, connected and resilient communities. www.ecoburbia.com.au

Environmentally Friendly Cremations. nd. Water cremation services. https://environmentallyfriendlycremations.com.au

Erem, C. 2021. Bank of Mum and Dad report 2020: Meet Australia's fifth biggest home loan lender. MOZO. https://mozo.com.au/home-loans/articles/bank-of-mum-and-and-dad-report-2020

Evans, L. 2019. 'The path of decisive change'. *Dumbo Feather Magazine*, vol. 59.

EveryAGE Counts. 2020. Ageism in the time of COVID-19. https://www.everyagecounts.org.au/ageism_in_the_time_of_covid_19

EveryAGE Counts. nd. The Pledge. https://www.everyagecounts.org.au/

Family Funeral Options. 2015. A summary of Australian funeral laws. http://www.allenfamilyfuneraloptions.com/a-summary-of-australian-funeral-laws/

Farmer, J., De Cotta, T. Knox, J. & Adler, V. 2020. Loneliness, social connection and COVID-19. Factsheet. Centre for Social Impact. https://www.csi.edu.au/media/uploads/csi-covid_factsheet_loneliness.pdf

Francis, S.L. 2018. *The Courage Way: Leading and living with integrity.* Berrett-Koehler, Oakland, CA.

Frankl. V. 2006. *Man's Search for Meaning.* Beacon Press, Boston, MA.

Frist, B. 2020. The effects of loneliness and social isolation With Dr. Julianne Holt-Lunstad. Podcast. A Second Opinion. https://asecondopinionpodcast.com/the-effects-of-loneliness-and-social-isolation-with-dr-julianne-holt-lunstad

Gathered Here. 2017. Everything end-of-life. www.gatheredhere.com.au

Gawande, A. 2015. *Being Mortal: Illness, medicine and what matters in the end.* Profile Books, London.

Good Reads. 2021. Albert Einstein: Quotable quotes. https://www.goodreads.com/quotes/38836-imagination-is-everything-it-is-the-preview-of-life-s-coming

Good Reads. 2021. Mahatma Gandhi: Quotable quotes. https://www.goodreads.com/quotes/518379-i-offer-you-peace-i-offer-you-love-i-offer

Graham, S. 2013. Take a street and build a community. TEDxPerth video. https://www.tedxperth.org/take-street-and-build-community

The GroundSwell Project. nd. Your emotional will. https://static1.squarespace.com/static/5f27363644ecfc2277942c88/t/5f4db8a3efa7cf4ad813cdd0/1598929075169/Emotional%2BWill.pdf

Hebb, M. 2018. *Let's Talk About Death Over Dinner.* Da Capo Press, New York.

The Henry Project. nd. Living together, living better. www.henryproject.com

Hillman, K. 2016. 'We're doing dying all wrong'. TEDxSydney video. https://tedxsydney.com/talk/were-doing-dying-all-wrong-ken-hillman

Hillman, K. 2017. *A Good Life To The End: Taking control of our inevitable journey through ageing and death.* Allen & Unwin, Crows Nest, NSW.

Homeshare Australia and New Zealand Alliance (HANZA). 2017. About Homeshare. https://homeshare.org.au/about-homeshare

Ibrahim, J. 2020. 'The inappropriate question'. Video. https://www.youtube.com/watch?v=30eXWq80E00

References

Jeong, S. 2019. The future of funerals: natural burial, home vigils, DIY coffins and more. *Choice*. https://www.choice.com.au/health-and-body/healthy-ageing/ageing-and-retirement/articles/funerals-investigation-the-future-of-funerals

Jones, A. & Silk, K. 2016. *Improving end-of-life care in Australia*. Deeble Institute. Summary: Paper 19. https://ahha.asn.au/system/files/docs/publications/summary_deeble_institute_issues_brief_no._19.pdf

Kaplan, D.B. & Berkman, B.J. 2019. *Religion and Spirituality in Older People*. MSD Manuals. Merck & Co., Kenilworth, NJ. https://www.msdmanuals.com/professional/geriatrics/social-issues-in-older-adults/religion-and-spirituality-in-older-adults

Khallouk, M., Lucas, T. & Gardiner, D. 2018. Healthy ageing. Development research report prepared for Department of Health. https://www.health.gov.au/sites/default/files/documents/2019/10/foi-request-951-healthy-ageing-developmental-research-report-healthy-ageing-developmental-research-report.pdf

Kittson, J. 2020. *We Need to Talk About Mum and Dad: A practical guide to parenting our ageing parents*. Pan Macmillan, Sydney.

Knippels, L. 2019. Hier hoor ik thuis (Here I belong). Blog post. https://het-ihc.nl/hier-hoor-ik-thuis/

Kollmorgen, A. 2016. Risky financial moves for over-50s: Reverse mortgages, home reversion schemes and SMSFs. *Choice*. https://www.choice.com.au/money/property/buying/articles/reverse-mortgages-and-home-reversion-schemes

Lawrence-Lightfoot, S. 2009. *The Third Chapter: Passion, risk and adventure in the 25 years after 50*. Sarah Crichton Books, New York.

Leider, R.J. & Shapiro, D.R. 2004. *Claiming Your Place at the Fire: Living the second half of your life on purpose*. Berrett-Koehler, San Francisco.

Leunig, M. 1990. *The Travelling Leunig*. Penguin, Melbourne.

Leunig, M. 2015. *Requiem*. https://www.leunig.com.au/works/recent-cartoons/225-requiem

Maccora, J., Ee, N., Hosking, D. & McCallum, J. 2020. Who Cares? Older Australians do. National Seniors, Canberra. https://nationalseniors.com.au/uploads/NSA-ResearchReport-Whocares.pdf

Mackay, H. 2013. *The Good Life: What makes a life worth living*. Pan Macmillan, Sydney.

Madigan, D. 2020. Cohousing for Ageing Well. https://www.madigan-architecture.com/portfolio/cohousing-for-ageing-well/#:~:text=Cohousing%20for%20Ageing%20Well%20(CHAW,City%20of%20Burnside%2C%20Town%20of

Manson, M. 2016. *The Art of Not Giving a F*ck: A counterintuitive approach to living a good life*. Pam MacMillan, Sydney.

McCamant, K. & Durrett, C. 2011. *Creating Cohousing: Building sustainable communities*. New Society, Gabriola Island, BC, Canada.

McCrindle Research. 2018. Future Care Study 2018, Absolute Care and Health. https://absolutecarehealth.com.au/assets/Uploads/Report-ACH-Future-Care-Study-2018-McCrindle.pdf

McCrindle Research. 2018. Older Australians not prepared for their future aged care. https://mccrindle.com.au/insights/blog/older-australians-not-prepared-for-their-future-age-care/

Metha, N. 2019. ServiceSpace. https://www.servicespace.org

Miller's Corner Cohousing Community. www.millerscorner.org

My Aged Care. nd. 'Find a provider'. https://www.myagedcare.gov.au/find-a-provider/

National Seniors Australia. 2021. Fairness in retirement income. https://nationalseniors.com.au/advocacy/current/fairness-in-retirement-income

National Seniors Productive Ageing Centre. 2012. Ageing baby boomers in Australia: Informing actions for better retirement. https://nationalseniors.com.au/uploads/201208_PACReport_Research_AgeingBoomersRetirement_0.pdf

Natural Death Advocacy Network. nd. Family led funerals. https://ndan.com.au/resources/family-led-funerals

O Tuama, P. 2019. The facts of life. *Dumbo Feather*, Issue 59-Second Quarter, 2019. St Kilda, Vic.

O'Shea (Pujji). J. 2007. The Precise Moment of Choice. *Follow Yourself Home*. Personal permission from author. www.wordremedies.co.nz

Osborne, C & Baldwin, C. 2020. '"Ageing in neighbourhood": what seniors want instead of retirement villages and how to achieve it', *The*

Conversation. https://theconversation.com/ageing-in-neighbourhood-what-seniors-want-instead-of-retirement-villages-and-how-to-achieve-it-138729

Palliative Care Australia. 2017. The economic benefits of home based palliative care and end-of-life care. Economic Research Note. https://palliativecare.org.au/wp-content/uploads/dlm_uploads/2017/07/PCA019_Economic-Research-Sheet_2a_Home-Based-Care.pdf

Palmer, P.J. 2004. *A Hidden Wholeness: The journey toward an undivided life.* Jossey-Bass, San Francisco.

Parliament of Australia, Senate Committee. 2018. Need for regulation of mobility scooters, also known as motorised wheelchairs. Report. https://www.aph.gov.au/Parliamentary_Business/Committees/Senate/Rural_and_Regional_Affairs_and_Transport/MobilityScooters/%20Report

Parsons, R. 2002. *The Heart of Success.* Hodder & Stoughton, London.

Pausch, R. 2018. The last lecture: Really achieving your childhood dreams. YouTube: https://www.youtube.com/watch?v=ji5_MqicxSo&vl=en

Pearson, M. & Wilson, H. 2014. *Sandplay and Symbol Work.* Australian Council for Educational Research, Melbourne, Victoria.

Plotkin, B. 2008. *Nature and the Human Soul: Cultivating wholeness and community in a fragmented world.* Finch Publishing Pty Limited, Lane Cover, NSW.

Potter, A. 2016. Lifting the lid on funerals. *Choice.* https://www.choice.com.au/health-and-body/healthy-ageing/ageing-and-retirement/articles/diy-funerals-and-coffins

Presencing Institute. 2012. U-Lab. www.presencing.org

Queensland University of Technology. 2021. End of Life Law in Australia: Euthanasia and assisted dying. https://end-of-life.qut.edu.au/euthanasia

Quibell, R. 2019. A precarious place: older women, housing insecurity & homelessness. *Women's Agenda.* https://womensagenda.com.au/life/a-precarious-place-older-women-housing-insecurity-homelessness/

Ratcliffe, J., Chen, G., Khadka, J., Kumaran, S., Hutchinson, C., Milte, R., Savvas, S. & Batchelor, F. 2020. Australia's aged care system: The quality-of-care experience and community expectations. Caring Futures Institute,

Flinders University, South Australia. https://agedcare.royalcommission.gov.au/sites/default/files/2021-02/qce-and-community-expectatons.pdf

Riedy, C., Wynne, L., Daly, M. & McKenna, K. 2017. *Cohousing for Seniors: Literature review*. Prepared for NSW Department of Family and Community Service and Office of Environment and Heritage, by Institute for Sustainable Futures, University of Technology, Sydney. https://www.academia.edu/33710122/Cohousing_for_Seniors_Literature_Review

Robertson, R. 2017. Why people in the 'blue zones' live longer than the rest of the world. *Healthline*. https://www.healthline.com/nutrition/blue-zones

Roy Morgan. 2020. What Australians think of ageing and aged care. Research Paper 4. A survey for the Royal Commission into Aged Care Quality and Safety. https://agedcare.royalcommission.gov.au/sites/default/files/2020-07/research_paper_4_-_what_australians_think_of_ageing_and_aged_care.pdf

Royal Commission into Aged Care Quality and Safety. 2019. Interim Report. https://agedcare.royalcommission.gov.au/publications/interim-report

Royal Commission into Aged Care Quality and Safety. 2019. Interim Report: Neglect. https://agedcare.royalcommission.gov.au/sites/default/files/2020-02/interim-report-volume-1.pdf

Royal Commission into Aged Care Quality and Safety. 2021. Final report._ https://agedcare.royalcommission.gov.au/publications/final-report

Royal Commission into Aged Care Quality and Safety. 2021. Final Report: Recommendations. https://agedcare.royalcommission.gov.au/sites/default/files/2021-03/final-report-recommendations.pdf

Rusinovic, K., Van Bochove, M. & Van de Sande, J. 2019. Senior co-housing in the Netherlands: Benefits and drawbacks for its residents. *International Journal of Environmental Research and Public Health*. Doi: https://www.mdpi.com/1660-4601/16/19/3776

Salzman, B. 2006. Myths and realities of ageing. *Care Management Journals* 7(3):141–50.

SBS OnDemand. 2021. *What does Australia really think about old people*. Documentary. https://www.sbs.com.au/ondemand/video/1929744451941/what-does-australia-really-think-about-old-people

References

Schachter-Shalomi, Z. & Miller, R.S. 2014. *From Age-ing to Sage-ing: A revolutionary approach to growing older.* Grand Central Publishing, New York.

Sheppard-Simms, E. 2020. As our cemeteries run out of space, composting burials could be the way of the future. *The Conversation.* https://theconversation.com/ashes-to-ashes-dust-to-compost-an-eco-friendly-burial-in-just-4-weeks-127794

South Australian Government, Department of Wellbeing and Ageing. 2020. State plan for ageing well 2020–2025. https://www.sahealth.sa.gov.au/wps/wcm/connect/f70e6b01-72ea-40e3-af7d-f3f641f24645/State+Plan+for+Ageing+Well+2020-2025.pdf?MOD=AJPERES&CACHEID=ROOTWORKSPACE-f70e6b01-72ea-40e3-af7d-f3f641f24645-niQvKCr

Suleman, R. & Bhatia, F. 2021. Intergenerational housing as a model for improving older-adult health, *BCMJ* 63(4):171–73. https://bcmj.org/articles/intergenerational-housing-model-improving-older-adult-health

Swerissen, H. & Duckett, S. 2014. *Dying well.* Grattan Institute, Report No. 2014-10. https://grattan.edu.au/wp-content/uploads/2014/09/815-dying-well.pdf

ThuisHuis. 2021. (Home House). www.thuishuis.org

Van der Laan, S. & Moerman, L. 2017. 'Consumers lose out in funeral industry lacking competition and regulation: study'. *The Conversation.* https://theconversation.com/consumers-lose-out-in-funeral-industry-lacking-competition-and-regulation-study-78031

Village to Village Network. 2021. Village model. https://www.vtvnetwork.org/content.aspx?page_id=22&club_id=691012&module_id=248578

Visontay, E. & Davey, M. 2021. 'Aged care leaders worry Morrison government's budget boost will not be enough'. *The Guardian.* https://www.theguardian.com/australia-news/2021/apr/20/aged-care-leaders-worry-morrison-governments-budget-boost-will-not-be-enough

Ware, B. 2019. *The Top Five Regrets of the Dying: A life transformed by the dearly departing.* Hay House Australia, Brighton-Le-Sands, NSW.

Ware, Bronnie. 2020. Regrets of the dying. Blog. https://bronnieware.com/blog/regrets-of-the-dying/

Waverton Hub. 2021. About Waverton Hub. http://www.wavertonhub.com.au

Web, E. & North, G. 2015. 'Suitable, affordable housing is key to our population ageing well'. *The Conversation.* https://theconversation.com/suitable-affordable-housing-is-key-to-our-population-aging-well-38644

Westendorp, R. & Schalkwijk, F.H. et.al. 2014. When vitality meets longevity: New strategies for health in later life. In T.B.L. Kirkwood & G. Cooper (eds), *Wellbeing: A complete reference guide. Vol. IV: Wellness in Later Life.* pp. 219–34. John Wiley & Sons, Ltd. Blackwell, Online Library: https://onlinelibrary.wiley.com/doi/full/10.1002/9781118539415.wbwell090

Where You Live Matters. 2021. What is rightsizing? https://www.whereyoulivematters.org/what-is-rightsizing/

Wildevuur, S., Van Dijk, D., Hammer-Jakobsen, T., Bjerre, M., Ayvari, A. & Lund, J. 2013. *Connect: Design for an Empathic Society.* BIS Publishers, Amsterdam.

Windsor, T.D., Curtis, R.G. & Luszcz, M.A. 2016. Social engagement in later life. In H. Kendig, P. McDonald & J. Piggott (eds), *Population Ageing and Australia's Future.* ANU Press, Canberra. http://press-files.anu.edu.au/downloads/press/n2121/pdf/ch09.pdf

World Health Organisation. 2020. Leaders speak out about their concerns about older people in the context of COVID-19. News. https://www.who.int/news-room/feature-stories/detail/leaders-speak-out-older-people-covid-19

World Health Organisation. 2021. Ageing: Healthy ageing and functional ability. https://www.who.int/westernpacific/news/q-a-detail/ageing-healthy-ageing-and-functional-ability

World Health Organisation. 2021. Ageism is a global challenge: UN. News. https://www.who.int/news/item/18-03-2021-ageism-is-a-global-challenge-un

World Health Organisation. 2021. Combatting ageism. https://www.who.int/teams/social-determinants-of-health/demographic-change-and-healthy-ageing/combatting-ageism

Young Institute. *Charlie and Marie: A tale of ageing.* YouTube video. https://www.youtube.com/watch?v=3qeK0q10crk

Endnotes

Preface

1   World Health Organisation. 2021. Ageing: Healthy ageing and functional ability. https://www.who.int/westernpacific/news/q-a-detail/ageing-healthy-ageing-and-functional-ability

Introduction

2   Australian Institute of Health and Welfare. 2018. Older Australians at a glance. https://www.aihw.gov.au/reports/older-people/older-australia-at-a-glance/contents/demographics-of-older-australians

3   The Australian Centre for Social Innovation. 2018. Future directions to support ageing well. Report prepared for the South Australian Government Office for the Ageing. https://www.sahealth.sa.gov.au/wps/wcm/connect/Public+Content/SA+Health+Internet/About+Us/Department+for+Health+and+Wellbeing/Office+for+Ageing+Well/Resources/Resources+about+ageing+well

4   The Australian Centre for Social Innovation. 2018. Future directions to support ageing well. Report prepared for the South Australian Government Office for the Ageing. https://www.sahealth.sa.gov.au/wps/wcm/connect/Public+Content/SA+Health+Internet/About+Us/Department+for+Health+and+Wellbeing/Office+for+Ageing+Well/Resources/Resources+about+ageing+well; and Roy Morgan. 2020. What

Australians think of ageing and aged care. Research Paper 4. A survey for the Royal Commission into Aged Care Quality and Safety. https://agedcare.royalcommission.gov.au/sites/default/files/2020-07/research_paper_4_-_what_australians_think_of_ageing_and_aged_care.pdf

5 Osborne, C & Baldwin, C. 2020. "'Ageing in neighbourhood': what senior want instead of retirement villages and how to achieve it', *The Conversation*. https://theconversation.com/ageing-in-neighbourhood-what-seniors-want-instead-of-retirement-villages-and-how-to-achieve-it-138729

6 McCrindle Research. 2018. Older Australians not prepared for their future aged care. https://mccrindle.com.au/insights/blog/older-australians-not-prepared-for-their-future-age-care/ and Khallouk, M., Lucas, T. & Gardiner, D. 2018. Healthy ageing. Development research report prepared for Department of Health. https://www.health.gov.au/sites/default/files/documents/2019/10/foi-request-951-healthy-ageing-developmental-research-report-healthy-ageing-developmental-research-report.pdf

Chapter 1. Home, Belonging and Community

7 Knippels, L. 2019. Hier hoor ik thuis (Here I belong). Blog post. https://het-ihc.nl/hier-hoor-ik-thuis/

8 Leider, R.J. & Shapiro, D.R. 2004. *Claiming Your Place at the Fire: Living the second half of your life on purpose.* Berrett-Koehler, San Francisco, p. 49.

9 Leider, R.J. & Shapiro, D.R. 2004. *Claiming Your Place at the Fire*, p. 51.

10 Leider, R.J. & Shapiro, D.R. 2004. *Claiming Your Place at the Fire*, p. 49.

11 Leider, R.J. & Shapiro, D.R. 2004. *Claiming Your Place at the Fire*, p. 53.

12 Adapted from Leider, R.J. & Shapiro, D.R. 2004. *Claiming Your Place at the Fire*, p. 53; and Durett, C. 2009. *The Senior Cohousing Handbook.* New Society, Gabriola Island, BC, Canada, p. 108.

Chapter 2. The Realities of Ageing

13 Department of Health, Victoria. 2021. Frailty. https://www.health.vic.gov.au/patient-care/frailty

14 Westendorp, R. & Schalkwijk, F.H. et.al. 2014. When vitality meets longevity: New strategies for health in later life. In T.B.L. Kirkwood & G. Cooper (eds), *Wellbeing: A complete reference guide. Vol. IV: Wellness in Later Life.* pp. 219–34. John Wiley & Sons Ltd. Blackwell, Online Library: https://onlinelibrary.wiley.com/doi/full/10.1002/9781118539415.wbwell090

15 You'll find a lot of information on the Independent Living Centres Australia website, and links to state centres: https://ilcaustralia.org.au/

16 Pausch, R. 2018. The last lecture: Really achieving your childhood dreams. YouTube: https://www.youtube.com/watch?v=ji5_MqicxSo&vl=en

17 Royal Commission into Aged Care Quality and Safety. 2019. Interim Report: Neglect. https://agedcare.royalcommission.gov.au/sites/default/files/2020-02/interim-report-volume-1.pdf

Chapter 3. Ageism

18 World Health Organisation. 2021. Ageism is a global challenge: UN. News. https://www.who.int/news/item/18-03-2021-ageism-is-a-global-challenge-un

19 World Health Organisation. 2021. Ageism is a global challenge: UN.

20 Jane Mussared, pers. comm.

21 Royal Commission into Aged Care Quality and Safety. 2019. Interim Report: Neglect. https://agedcare.royalcommission.gov.au/sites/default/files/2020-02/interim-report-volume-1.pdf

22 Australian Human Rights Commission. 2019. Age Discrimination: exposing the hidden barrier for mature age workers (2010). https://humanrights.gov.au/our-work/age-discrimination/publications/age-discrimination-exposing-hidden-barrier-mature-age

23 The Benevolent Society. 2017. The drivers of ageism. Summary Report. www.benevolent.org.au.

24 Salzman, B. 2006. Myths and realities of ageing. *Care Management Journals* 7(3):141–50.

25 EveryAGE Counts. 2020. Ageism in the time of COVID-19. https://www.everyagecounts.org.au/ageism_in_the_time_of_covid_19

26 The Benevolent Society. 2017. The drivers of ageism, p. 16.
27 Applewhite, A. 2019. *This Chair Rocks: A manifesto against ageism*. Celadon Books, New York.
28 Applewhite, A. 2017. 'Let's end ageism'. TED2017. https://www.ted.com/talks/ashton_applewhite_let_s_end_ageism
29 Metha, N. 2019. ServiceSpace. https://www.servicespace.org
30 Maccora, J., Ee, N., Hosking, D. & McCallum, J. 2020. *Who Cares? Older Australians do*. National Seniors, Canberra. https://nationalseniors.com.au/uploads/NSA-ResearchReport-Whocares.pdf
31 SBS OnDemand. 2021. What does Australia really think about old people. Series. https://www.sbs.com.au/programs/what-does-australia-really-think-about
32 The Benevolent Society. 2017. The drivers of ageism, p. 27.
33 Quoted in Leider, R.J. & Shapiro, D.R. 2004. *Claiming Your Place at the Fire: Living the second half of your life on purpose*. Berrett-Koehler, San Francisco, p. 103.

Chapter 4. Money Matters

34 Swerissen, H. & Duckett, S. 2014. *Dying well*. Grattan Institute, Report No. 2014-10. https://grattan.edu.au/wp-content/uploads/2014/09/815-dying-well.pdf
35 The Australian Centre for Social Innovation. 2017. Investing in systemic impacts to improve end of life outcomes. Summary report. https://www.tacsi.org.au/wp-content/uploads/2018/07/Systemic-Impact-in-End-of-Life_report-updated-02.07.2018.pdf
36 Australian Instate of Health and Welfare. 2021. Interfaces between aged care and health systems in Australia – where do older Australians die? https://www.gen-agedcaredata.gov.au/www_aihwgen/media/2021-Interfaces-reports/Interfaces-between-the-aged-care-and-health-systems-in-Australia-where-do-older-Australians-die.pdf
37 Brodsky, J. Grey, F. & Sinclair, S. 2018. 'For Australians to have a choice of growing old at home, here is what needs to change'. *The Conversation*. https://theconversation.com/for-australians-to-have-the-choice-of-growing-old-at-home-here-is-what-needs-to-change-91488

ENDNOTES

38   National Seniors Australia. 2021. https://nationalseniors.com.au/advocacy/current/fairness-in-retirement-income

39   McCrindle Research. 2018. Older Australians not prepared for their future aged care. https://mccrindle.com.au/insights/blog/older-australians-not-prepared-for-their-future-age-care/

40   Australian Housing and Urban Research Institute (AHURI). 2021. Better supporting older Australians to age in place. https://www.ahuri.edu.au/research/ahuri-briefs/better-supporting-older-australians-to-age-in-place

41   Palliative Care Australia. 2017. The economic benefits of home based palliative care and end-of-life care. Economic Research Note. https://palliativecare.org.au/wp-content/uploads/dlm_uploads/2017/07/PCA019_Economic-Research-Sheet_2a_Home-Based-Care.pdf

42   Lawrence-Lightfoot, S. 2009. *The Third Chapter: Passion, risk and adventure in the 25 years after 50*. Sarah Crichton Books, New York, p. xii.

43   National Seniors Productive Ageing Centre. 2012. Ageing baby boomers in Australia: Informing actions for better retirement. https://nationalseniors.com.au/uploads/201208_PACReport_Research_AgeingBoomersRetirement_0.pdf

44   Australian Government, Department of Social Services. 2019. Age pension. https://www.dss.gov.au/seniors/benefits-payments/age-pension

45   Australian Bureau of Statistics. 2011. Retirement and retirement intentions. Cat no: 6238.0. ABS, Canberra. https://www.abs.gov.au/statistics/labour/employment-and-unemployment/retirement-and-retirement-intentions-australia/latest-release#:~:text=55%25%20of%20people%20over%2055,to%20retire%20is%2065.5%20years

46   National Seniors Productive Ageing Centre. 2012. Ageing Baby Boomers in Australia: Informing Actions for Better Retirement.

47   National Seniors Productive Ageing Centre. 2012. Ageing Baby Boomers in Australia: Informing Actions for Better Retirement.

48   Butler, M. 2015. *Advanced Australia: The politics of ageing*. Melbourne University Press, Carlton, Vic., p. 90.

49 Erem, C. 2021. Bank of Mum and Dad report 2020: Meet Australia's fifth biggest home loan lender. MOZO. https://mozo.com.au/home-loans/articles/bank-of-mum-and-and-dad-report-2020

50 Australian Broadcasting Corporation. 2019. 'Retraining won't keep older workers from choosing to retire'. https://www.abc.net.au/news/2019-11-20/retraining-wont-keep-older-workers-from-choosing-to-retire/11720482

51 Brown, B. 2020. 'COVID-19 puts a squeeze on older Australians' finances'. *Financial Review*. https://www.afr.com/wealth/personal-finance/covid-19-puts-squeeze-on-older-australians-finances-20200406-p54hgn

52 Royal Commission into Aged Care Quality and Safety. 2021. Final report. https://agedcare.royalcommission.gov.au/publications/final-report

53 Australian Government, Department of Health. 2021. Budget delivers $17.7 billion for once a generation change to aged care in Australia. https://www.health.gov.au/news/budget-delivers-177-billion-for-once-in-a-generation-change-to-aged-care-in-australia

54 Australian Government, Department of Health. 2021. Budget delivers $17.7 billion.

55 Visontay, E. & Davey, M. 2021. 'Aged care leaders worry Morrison government's budget boost will not be enough'. *The Guardian*. https://www.theguardian.com/australia-news/2021/apr/20/aged-care-leaders-worry-morrison-governments-budget-boost-will-not-be-enough

56 Coorey, P. & McIlroy, T. 2021. 'PM mulls aged care tax'. *Financial Review*. https://www.afr.com/politics/federal/pm-mulls-aged-care-tax-20210301-p576m8

57 Dawson, E., 2019. The economic impacts of ageism. Speech to the COTA Australia National Policy Forum. https://percapita.org.au/2019/06/17/speech-the-economic-impacts-of-ageism/

58 Centre for Ageing Better. 2019. The state of ageing in 2019: Adding life to our years. https://www.ageing-better.org.uk/sites/default/files/2019-11/The-State-of-Ageing-2019-Adding-life-to-our-years.pdf

59 The Australian Centre for Social Innovation. 2018. Future directions to support ageing well. Report prepared for the South Australian

Endnotes

Government Office for the Ageing. https://www.sahealth.sa.gov.au/wps/wcm/connect/Public+Content/SA+Health+Internet/About+Us/Department+for+Health+and+Wellbeing/Office+for+Ageing+Well/Resources/Resources+about+ageing+well, p.15.

60 Also consider other independent sources of information, such as Choice, (e.g. in regards to equity in the family home: https://www.choice.com.au/money/property/buying/articles/reverse-mortgages-and-home-reversion-schemes) and check on things like how long the business has been in existence, who finances it, and who pays the consultant or advisor.

Chapter 5. Care and Care Support

61 McCrindle Research. 2018. Future Care Study 2018, Absolute Care and Health. https://absolutecarehealth.com.au/assets/Uploads/Report-ACH-Future-Care-Study-2018-McCrindle.pdf

62 McCrindle Research. 2018. Future Care Study 2018, Absolute Care and Health., p. 6.

63 Ratcliffe, J., Chen, G., Khadka, J., Kumaran, S., Hutchinson, C., Milte, R., Savvas, S. & Batchelor, F. 2020. *Australia's aged care system: The quality-of-care experience and community expectations.* Caring Futures Institute, Flinders University, South Australia. https://agedcare.royalcommission.gov.au/sites/default/files/2021-02/qce-and-community-expectatons.pdf

64 Wildevuur, S., Van Dijk, D., Hammer-Jakobsen, T., Bjerre, M., Ayvari, A. & Lund, J. 2013. *Connect: Design for an Empathic Society.* BIS Publishers, Amsterdam, p. 16.

65 The Young Institute. *Charlie and Marie: A tale of ageing.* YouTube video. https://www.youtube.com/watch?v=3qeK0q10crk

66 McCrindle Research. 2018. Older Australians not prepared for their future aged care. https://mccrindle.com.au/insights/blog/older-australians-not-prepared-for-their-future-age-care/

67 Kittson, J. 2020. *We Need to Talk About Mum and Dad: A practical guide to parenting our ageing parents.* Pan Macmillan, Sydney.

68 Durett, C. 2009. *The Senior Cohousing Handbook*. New Society, Gabriola Island, BC, Canada, pp. 119–127.
69 Robertson, R. 2017. Why people in the 'blue zones' live longer than the rest of the world. *Healthline*. https://www.healthline.com/nutrition/blue-zones
70 Buettner, D. 2016. Power 9: Reverse engineering longevity. https://www.bluezones.com/2016/11/power-9/
71 Village to Village Network. 2021. Village model. https://www.vtvnetwork.org/content.aspx?page_id=22&club_id=691012&module_id=248578
72 Waverton Hub. 2021. About Waverton Hub. http://www.wavertonhub.com.au
73 Connect Victoria Park. 2021. https://www.connectvictoriapark.org/
74 Waverton Hub. 2021. About Waverton Hub.
75 Cottam, Hilary. 2018. *Radical Help: How we can remake the relationships between us and revolutionise the welfare state*. Virago. London.
76 For more information about requirements for registration, see Aged Care Quality and Safety Commission: 'Becoming an approved aged care provider', 2021, https://www.agedcarequality.gov.au/providers/becoming-approved-aged-care-provider; and *Guidance for Applicants Seeking Approval to Provide Aged Care*. Booklet, 2020. https://www.agedcarequality.gov.au/sites/default/files/media/guidance_for_applicants_seeking_approval_to_provide_aged_care_0.pdf
77 My Aged Care. nd. 'Find a provider'. https://www.myagedcare.gov.au/find-a-provider/
78 Royal Commission into Aged Care Quality and Safety. 2019. Interim Report: Neglect. https://agedcare.royalcommission.gov.au/sites/default/files/2020-02/interim-report-volume-1.pdf
79 Royal Commission into Aged Care Quality and Safety. 2021. Final Report: Recommendations. https://agedcare.royalcommission.gov.au/sites/default/files/2021-03/final-report-recommendations.pdf
80 Wells, Anika. 2022. Department of Health and Aged Care. 'Getting In-Home Care back on track', media release, 28 July. https://www.health.

gov.au/ministers/the-hon-anika-wells-mp/media/getting-in-home-care-back-on-track

81 Wildevuur, S., Van Dijk, D., Hammer-Jakobsen, T., Bjerre, M., Ayvari, A. & Lund, J. 2013. *Connect*, p. 203.

Chapter 6. The Importance of Social Connections

82 Palmer, P.J. 2004. *A Hidden Wholeness: The journey toward an undivided life*. Jossey-Bass, San Francisco, pp. 54–55.

83 Australian Institute of Health and Welfare. 2019. Social isolation and loneliness. https://www.aihw.gov.au/reports/australias-welfare/social-isolation-and-loneliness

84 Centre for Ageing Better. 2019. The state of ageing in 2019: Adding life to our years. https://www.ageing-better.org.uk/sites/default/files/2019-11/The-State-of-Ageing-2019-Adding-life-to-our-years.pdf

85 Frist, B. 2020. The effects of loneliness and social isolation With Dr. Julianne Holt-Lunstad. Podcast. A Second Opinion. https://asecondopinionpodcast.com/the-effects-of-loneliness-and-social-isolation-with-dr-julianne-holt-lunstad

86 Windsor, T.D., Curtis, R.G. & Luszcz, M.A. 2016. Social engagement in later life. In H. Kendig, P. McDonald & J. Piggott (eds), *Population Ageing and Australia's Future*. ANU Press, Canberra. http://press-files.anu.edu.au/downloads/press/n2121/pdf/ch09.pdf

87 Farmer, J., De Cotta, T. Knox, J. & Adler, V. 2020. Loneliness, social connection and COVID-19. Factsheet. Centre for Social Impact. https://www.csi.edu.au/media/uploads/csi-covid_factsheet_loneliness.pdf

88 Pearson, M. & Wilson, H. 2014. *Sandplay and Symbol Work*. Australian Council for Educational Research, Melbourne, Victoria, p. 62.

89 World Health Organisation. 2020. Leaders speak out about their concerns about older people in the context of COVID-19. News. https://www.who.int/news-room/feature-stories/detail/leaders-speak-out-older-people-covid-19

90 Carter, C. 2017. *How to Handle a Toxic Relationship*. The Greater Good Science Center. https://greatergood.berkeley.edu/article/item/how_to_handle_a_toxic_relationship

91 Wildevuur, S., Van Dijk, D., Hammer-Jakobsen, T., Bjerre, M., Ayvari, A. & Lund, J. 2013. *Connect: Design for an Empathic Society*. BIS Publishers, Amsterdam, p. 200.
92 Graham, S. 2013. Take a street and build a community. TEDxPerth video. https://www.tedxperth.org/take-street-and-build-community
93 Ecoburbia. 2018. Creating more sustainable, connected and resilient communities. www.ecoburbia.com.au

Chapter 7. Emerging and Established Housing Models

94 Australian Bureau of Statistics. 2016. Disability, ageing and carers, Australia: Summary of findings, 2015. Cat no: 4430.0. ABS, Canberra. https://www.abs.gov.au/ausstats/abs@.nsf/Lookup/4430.0main+features302015
95 Australian Bureau of Statistics. 2017. Census of population and housing: Reflecting Australia – Stories from the census, 2016. Cat no: 2071.0. https://www.abs.gov.au/ausstats/abs@.nsf/Lookup/by%20Subject/2071.0~2016~Main%20Features~Ageing%20Population~14
96 Quibell, R. 2019. A precarious place: older women, housing insecurity & homelessness. *Women's Agenda*. https://womensagenda.com.au/life/a-precarious-place-older-women-housing-insecurity-homelessness/
97 Web, E. & North, G. 2015. 'Suitable, affordable housing is key to our population ageing well'. *The Conversation*. https://theconversation.com/suitable-affordable-housing-is-key-to-our-population-aging-well-38644
98 Australian Institute of Health and Welfare. 2020. Housing assistance in Australia 2020. https://www.aihw.gov.au/reports/housing-assistance/housing-assistance-in-australia-2020/contents/priority-groups-and-waiting-lists#wait-times
99 Brodsky, J. Grey, F. & Sinclair, S. 2018. 'For Australians to have a choice of growing old at home, here is what needs to change'. *The Conversation*. https://theconversation.com/for-australians-to-have-the-choice-of-growing-old-at-home-here-is-what-needs-to-change-91488
100 Automobility. 2021. Road rules for wheelchair users. https://automobility.com.au/road-rules-for-wheelchair-users. In 2018 a Senate Committee considered the use of mobility scooters and motorised

wheelchairs; its report: Need for regulation of mobility scooters, also known as motorised wheelchairs, is available at https://www.aph.gov.au/Parliamentary_Business/Committees/Senate/Rural_and_Regional_Affairs_and_Transport/MobilityScooters/%20Report

101 Centers for Disease Control and Prevention. Morbidity and Mortality. Nonfatal Bathroom Injuries Among Persons Aged > 15 years, United States 2008. *Weekly Report*, 10 June 2011 / 60 (22), 729–33. https://www.cdc.gov/mmwr/preview/mmwrhtml/mm6022a1.htm

102 Quoted in Where You Live Matters. 2021. What is rightsizing? https://www.whereyoulivematters.org/what-is-rightsizing/

103 Centre for Excellence in Universal Design. 2020. *What is Universal Design*. Dublin, Ireland. http://universaldesign.ie/What-is-Universal-Design/

104 South Australian Government, Department of Wellbeing and Ageing. 2020. State plan for ageing well 2020–2025. https://www.sahealth.sa.gov.au/wps/wcm/connect/f70e6b01-72ea-40e3-af7d-f3f641f24645/State+Plan+for+Ageing+Well+2020-2025.pdf?MOD=AJPERES&CACHEID=ROOTWORKSPACE-f70e6b01-72ea-40e3-af7d-f3f641f24645-niQvKCr

105 Australian Institute of Health and Welfare. 2019. Social isolation and loneliness. https://www.aihw.gov.au/reports/australias-welfare/social-isolation-and-loneliness

106 Riedy, C., Wynne, L., Daly, M. & McKenna, K. 2017. *Cohousing for Seniors: Literature review*. Prepared for NSW Department of Family and Community Service and Office of Environment and Heritage, by Institute for Sustainable Futures, University of Technology, Sydney. https://www.academia.edu/33710122/Cohousing_for_Seniors_Literature_Review

107 Riedy, C., Wynne, L., Daly, M. & McKenna, K. 2017. *Cohousing for Seniors: Literature review*. https://www.academia.edu/en/33710122/Cohousing_for_Seniors_Literature_Review

108 Brenton, M. 2010. Potential benefits of cohousing for older people. A literature review. *Elderwoman*. http://www.elderwoman.org/potential_cohousing_benefits.pdf; De Campo, J., Jones, K., McPhee, L.

& Vanstone, C. 2021. *The Future of Home*. The Australian Centre for Social Innovation, Adelaide. https://tacsi.org.au/future-of-home/; and Suleman, R. & Bhatia, F. 2021. Intergenerational housing as a model for improving older-adult health, *BCMJ* 63(4):171–73. https://bcmj.org/articles/intergenerational-housing-model-improving-older-adult-health. See also the Resources list for this chapter.

109 Collaborative Housing. 2019. The Shedders. https://www.collaborativehousing.org.au/stories-the-shedders

110 The AGEncy Project. 2021. www.agencycohcom.org

111 Homeshare Australia and New Zealand Alliance (HANZA). 2017. About Homeshare. https://homeshare.org.au/about-homeshare

112 The Henry Project. nd. Living together, living better. www.henryproject.com

113 McCamant, K. & Durrett, C. 2011. *Creating Cohousing: Building sustainable communities*. New Society, Gabriola Island, BC, Canada, p. 39.

114 McCamant, K. & Durrett, C. 2011. *Creating Cohousing: Building sustainable communities*.

115 Cohousing Australia. 2021. Cohousing Architecture Australia. https://cohousing.com.au/; and Cohousing Australia. Facebook page. https://www.facebook.com/cohousingaustralia

116 Suleman, R. & Bhatia, F. 2021. Intergenerational housing as a model for improving older-adult health, *BCMJ* 63(4):171–73. https://bcmj.org/articles/intergenerational-housing-model-improving-older-adult-health

117 Miller's Corner Cohousing Community. www.millerscorner.org.au

118 ThuisHuis. 2021. (Home House). www.thuishuis.org

119 Madigan, D. 2020. Cohousing for Ageing Well. https://www.madigan-architecture.com/portfolio/cohousing-for-ageing-well/#:~:text=Cohousing%20for%20Ageing%20Well%20(CHAW,City%20of%20Burnside%2C%20Town%20of

120 They are: the Office for Ageing Well (SA Health Department), the South Australian State Planning Commission, the SA Department for Infrastructure, and four inner-Adelaide councils: the cities of Unley, Burnside and Prospect and the Town of Walkerville.

121 Brodsky, J. Grey, F. & Sinclair, S. 2018. 'For Australians to have a choice of growing old at home, here is what needs to change'. *The Conversation*. https://theconversation.com/for-australians-to-have-the-choice-of-growing-old-at-home-here-is-what-needs-to-change-91488

Chapter 8. Living Life with Meaning and Purpose

122 Albom, M. 1997. *Tuesdays with Morrie*. Hodder Headline Australia, Rydalmere, NSW.
123 Plotkin, B. 2008. *Nature and the Human Soul: Cultivating wholeness and community in a fragmented world*. Finch Publishing Pty Limited, Lane Cover, NSW. Chapter 11.
124 Barnes, S.F. 2011. Third age: The golden years of adulthood. *California Booming*. San Diego State University. http://calbooming.sdsu.edu/documents/TheThirdAge.pdf
125 Frankl. V. 2006. *Man's Search for Meaning*. Beacon Press, Boston, MA.
126 Mackay, H. 2013. *The Good Life: What makes a life worth living*. Pan Macmillan, Sydney, p. 1.
127 Ware, Bronnie. 2020. Regrets of the dying. Blog. https://bronnieware.com/blog/regrets-of-the-dying/
128 Ware, B. 2019. *The Top Five Regrets of the Dying: A life transformed by the dearly departing*. Hay House Australia, Brighton-Le-Sands, NSW.
129 Ware, Bronnie. 2020. Regrets of the dying. Blog.
130 Bound Alberti. F. 2019. *A Biography of Loneliness: The history of an emotion*. Oxford University Press, p. 225.
131 Denborough, D. 2014. *Retelling the Stories of our Lives: Everyday narrative therapy to draw inspiration and transform experience*. W.W. Norton & Co., New York.
132 Cited in Bound Alberti. F. 2019. *A Biography of Loneliness*, p. 141.
133 Royal Commission into Aged Care Quality and Safety. 2019. Interim Report. https://agedcare.royalcommission.gov.au/publications/interim-report
134 Frankl. V. 2006. *Man's Search for Meaning*, pp. 151, 148.
135 O'Shea (Pujji). J. 2007. *Follow Yourself Home*. www.wordremedies.co.nz

136 Kaplan, D.B. & Berkman, B.J. 2019. *Religion and Spirituality in Older People*. MSD Manuals. Merck & Co., Kenilworth, NJ. https://www.msdmanuals.com/professional/geriatrics/social-issues-in-older-adults/religion-and-spirituality-in-older-adults

137 From Cameron, J. 1995. *The Artist Way*. Pan Books, London, p. 89.

138 Quoted in Dowrick, S. 2010. *Seeking the Sacred: Transforming our view of ourselves and one another*. Allen & Unwin, Crows Nest, NSW, p. 287.

Chapter 9. Planning for End of Life

139 Australian Government, Department of Health. 2019. Advance care planning. https://www.health.gov.au/health-topics/palliative-care/planning-your-palliative-care/advance-care-planning

140 Jones, A. & Silk, K. 2016. *Improving end-of-life care in Australia*. Deeble Institute. Summary: Paper 19. https://ahha.asn.au/system/files/docs/publications/summary_deeble_institute_issues_brief_no._19.pdf

141 Buckley, A. 2019. Pushing up the daisies workshop. Blog. https://www.ourfamilycelebrant.com.au/category/pushing-up-daisies-workshop/

142 Hebb, M. 2018. *Let's Talk About Death Over Dinner*. Da Capo Press, New York, pp. vii–viii.

143 Swerissen, H. & Duckett, S. 2014. *Dying well*. Grattan Institute, Report No. 2014-10. https://grattan.edu.au/wp-content/uploads/2014/09/815-dying-well.pdf

144 Hillman, K. 2016. 'We're doing dying all wrong'. TEDxSydney video. https://tedxsydney.com/talk/were-doing-dying-all-wrong-ken-hillman/

145 Gawande, A. 2014. *Being Mortal: Illness, medicine and what matters in the end*. Profile Books, London, p. 149.

146 Gawande, A. 2014. *Being Mortal*, p. 155.

147 Advance Care Planning Australia. 2021. https://www.advancecareplanning.org.au/

148 Australian Government, Department of Health. 2019. Advance care planning. https://www.health.gov.au/health-topics/palliative-care/planning-your-palliative-care/advance-care-planning

Endnotes

149 Advance Care Planning Australia. 2015. 'Advance Care Planning 1: Starting the conversation'. Video. https://www.youtube.com/watch?v=QagbgTYCtMY

150 Australian Government Organ and Tissue Authority. 2021. 'Register as a donor today'. https://donatelife.gov.au/register-donor-today

151 The GroundSwell Project. nd. Your emotional will. https://static1.squarespace.com/static/5f27363644ecfc2277942c88/t/5f4db8a3efa7cf4ad813cdd0/1598929075169/Emotional%2BWill.pdf

152 To find out more about what palliative care has to offer, contact Palliative Care Australia on 02 6232 0700 or via email pca@palliativecare.org.au. Find your local palliative care organisation under 'Members'. The website also contains other useful resource material: https://palliativecare.org.au/

153 Australian Doula College. 2020. https://www.australiandoulacollege.com.au/

154 Queensland University of Technology. 2021. End of Life Law in Australia: Euthanasia and assisted dying. https://end-of-life.qut.edu.au/euthanasia

Chapter 10. Planning for Your Funeral

155 Browne. K. 2020. What to do when someone dies: A helpful checklist of the necessary processes when someone close to you passes away. *Choice*. https://www.choice.com.au/health-and-body/healthy-ageing/ageing-and-retirement/articles/what-to-do-when-someone-dies. You can also contact Choice via phone: 1800 069 552.

156 Browne. K. 2020. What to do when someone dies.

157 Natural Death Advocacy Network. nd. Family led funerals. https://ndan.com.au/resources/family-led-funerals. There is no phone number provided, and email is via their webpage only.

158 Gathered Here. 2017. Everything end-of-life. www.gatheredhere.com.au. There is no phone number provided, and email is via their webpage only. *Choice* offers a word of caution: 'As with comparison sites for energy, insurance and finance, a "free" service such as Gathered Here is unlikely to give you the full picture, listing only a portion of the market. And because funeral homes, not consumers, fund the comparison site, you

can see how Gathered Here might be financially compelled to keep its paying members happy.' It is important to ask such questions. See the *Choice* article: Jeong, S. 2019. The future of funerals: natural burial, home vigils, DIY coffins and more. https://www.choice.com.au/health-and-body/healthy-ageing/ageing-and-retirement/articles/funerals-investigation-the-future-of-funerals

159 Potter, A. 2016. Lifting the lid on funerals. *Choice*. https://www.choice.com.au/health-and-body/healthy-ageing/ageing-and-retirement/articles/diy-funerals-and-coffins

160 Browne. K. 2020. What to do when someone dies.

161 Browne. K. 2020. What to do when someone dies.

162 Natural Death Advocacy Network. nd. Family led funerals.

163 Family Funeral Options. 2015. A summary of Australian funeral laws. http://www.allenfamilyfuneraloptions.com/a-summary-of-australian-funeral-laws/

164 Van der Laan, S. & Moerman, L. 2017. 'Consumers lose out in funeral industry lacking competition and regulation: study'. *The Conversation*. https://theconversation.com/consumers-lose-out-in-funeral-industry-lacking-competition-and-regulation-study-78031

165 Aquamation International. 2021. Aquamation. http://www.aquamationindustries.com/what-is-alkaline-hydrolysis

166 For details see Environmentally Friendly Cremations. nd. Water cremation services. https://environmentallyfriendlycremations.com.au

167 Sheppard-Simms, E. 2020. As our cemeteries run out of space, composting burials could be the way of the future. *The Conversation*. https://theconversation.com/ashes-to-ashes-dust-to-compost-an-eco-friendly-burial-in-just-4-weeks-127794

168 O Tuama, P. 2019. The facts of life. *Dumbo Feather*, Issue 59-Second Quarter, 2019. St Kilda, Vic., p. 52.

Chapter 11. Courage to Change: To Live, Age and Die Well

169 Manson, M. 2016. *The Art of Not Giving a F*ck: A counterintuitive approach to living a good life*. Pam MacMillan, Sydney, p. 54.

170 Hillman, K. 2017. *A Good Life To The End: Taking control of our inevitable journey through ageing and death.* Allen & Unwin, Crows Nest, NSW, p. 19.
171 Francis, S.L. 2018. *The Courage Way: Leading and living with integrity.* Berrett-Koehler, Oakland, CA, p. 8.
172 Francis, S.L. 2018. *The Courage Way*, p. 8.
173 Gawande, A. 2014. *Being Mortal*, p. 232.
174 Quoted in Dietz, J. 2000. *Yes, You Can: Go beyond physical adversity and live life to its fullest.* Demos Medical, New York, p. 93.
175 Francis, S.L. 2018. *The Courage Way: Leading and living with integrity.* Berrett-Koehler, Oakland, CA, p. 9.
176 World Health Organisation. 2021. Combatting ageism. https://www.who.int/teams/social-determinants-of-health/demographic-change-and-healthy-ageing/combatting-ageism
177 Francis, S.L. 2018. *The Courage Way*, p. 10.
178 EveryAGE Counts. nd. The Pledge. https://www.everyagecounts.org.au/, viewed 27 April 2021; email available on website only.
179 Francis, S.L. 2018. *The Courage Way*, p. 103.
180 Francis, S.L. 2018. *The Courage Way*, pp. 11–12.
181 Evans, L. 2019. 'The path of decisive change'. *Dumbo Feather Magazine* vol. 59, p. 9.
182 Francis, S.L. 2018. *The Courage Way*, p. 14.
183 Good Reads. 2021. Albert Einstein: Quotable quotes. https://www.goodreads.com/quotes/38836-imagination-is-everything-it-is-the-preview-of-life-s-coming

Conclusion. On Your Way

184 Leider, R.J. & Shapiro, D.R. 2004. *Claiming Your Place at the Fire: Living the second half of your life on purpose.* Berrett-Koehler, San Francisco, pp. 51–52.
185 Palmer, P.J. 2004. *A Hidden Wholeness: The journey toward an undivided life.* Jossey-Bass, San Francisco, p. 173.

www.ingramcontent.com/pod-product-compliance
Lightning Source LLC
Chambersburg PA
CBHW050309010526
44107CB00055B/2161